MATHS & ENGLISH FOR
RETAIL

Graduated exercises and practice exam

Andrew Spencer and Carole Vella

CENGAGE
Learning

Australia • Brazil • Japan • Korea • Mexico • Singapore • Spain • United Kingdom • United States

Maths & English for Retail

Andrew Spencer and Carole Vella

Publishing Director: Linden Harris

Publisher: Lucy Mills

Development Editor: Claire Napoli

Editorial Assistant: Lauren Darby

Production Editor: Alison Burt

Manufacturing Buyer: Eyvett Davis

Typesetter: Cambridge Publishing Management Limited

Cover design: HCT Creative

While the publisher has taken all reasonable care in the preparation of this book, the publisher makes no representation, express or implied, with regard to the accuracy of the information contained in this book and cannot accept any legal responsibility or liability for any errors or omissions from the book or the consequences thereof.

Products and services that are referred to in this book may be either trademarks and/or registered trademarks of their respective owners. The publishers and author/s make no claim to these trademarks. The publisher does not endorse, and accepts no responsibility or liability for, incorrect or defamatory content contained in hyperlinked material.

For product information and technology assistance, contact **emea.info@cengage.com**.

For permission to use material from this text or product, and for permission queries, email **emea.permissions@cengage.com**.

This work is adapted from *Pre Apprenticeship: Maths & Literacy Series* by Andrew Spencer published by Cengage Learning Australia Pty Limited © 2010.

British Library Cataloguing-in-Publication Data
A catalogue record for this book is available from the British Library.

ISBN: 978-1-4080-8308-6

Cengage Learning EMEA Cheriton House, North Way, Andover, Hampshire, SP10 5BE United Kingdom

Cengage Learning products are represented in Canada by Nelson Education Ltd.

For your lifelong learning solutions, visit **www.cengage.co.uk**

Purchase your next print book, e-book or e-chapter at **www.cengagebrain.com**

Printed in Greece by Bakis
1 2 3 4 5 6 7 8 9 10 – 15 14 13

Maths & English for Retail

Contents

Introduction

Functional skills are essential skills in English and mathematics that enable everyone to deal with the practical problems and challenges of life – at home, in education and at work. They are essential to all our lives. For example, they help us recognize good value deals when making purchases, in writing an effective application letter, or when using the internet to access local services or online banking. They are about using English, mathematics and ICT in everyday situations.

Functional skills are a key to success. They open doors to learning, to life and to work. These skills are valued by employers and further education institutions and are a platform on which to build other employability skills. Better functional skills can mean a better future – as learners or as employees.

Functional skills are an essential part of the secondary curriculum. They are embedded in the revised Programmes of Study for English, mathematics and ICT at Key Stage 3 and Key Stage 4, and in the revised GCSE subject criteria for these subjects. They are a mandatory component of Diplomas, the Foundation Learning Tier (FLT) and Apprenticeships. They will also be available as stand-alone qualifications for young people and adults. Functional skills are based on a problem-solving approach and should be developed in a practical way through discussion, thinking and explanation, across the whole 11–19 curriculum.

It is therefore important to recognize and promote awareness that functional skills are essential for:

- getting the most from education and training

- the personal development of all young people and adults

- independence – enabling learners to manage in a variety of situations

- developing employability skills

- giving people a sound basis for further learning.

The implications for teaching and learning are significant and will need to be introduced gradually and thoughtfully, but they do not threaten aspects of existing good practice. Helping learners to become more 'functional' is supported by existing practices including:

- a focus on applied learning

- learner-centred approaches

- active learning and a problem-centred approach

- partnership learning

- assessment for learning.

The skills in this book are tailored to a student working in Retail by developing their employability skills. Commonly used industry terms are introduced so that students have a basic understanding of terminology that they will encounter in the workplace environment (words that are in the glossary appear in **bold** the first time they are used). Students who can complete this workbook and reach a higher outcome in all topics will have achieved the goal of this resource.

About the authors

Andrew Spencer has studied education both within Australia and overseas. He has a Bachelor of Education, as well as a Masters of Science in which he specialized in teacher education. Andrew has extensive experience in teaching secondary mathematics throughout New South Wales and South Australia for well over fifteen years. He has taught a range of subject areas, including Maths, English, Science, Classics, Physical Education and Technical Studies. His sense of the importance of practical mathematics has continued to develop with the range of subject areas he has taught in.

Carole Vella studied Business Studies in the UK. She has a Bachelor of Arts in Business Management and Information Technology, as well as a Masters of Business Administration. Carole has extensive experience in teaching and examining Business Studies in the UK for over 12 years. She has taught a range of subject areas, including Business Administration, Retail, Marketing, Human Resources and Economics.

Acknowledgements

Andrew Spencer:
>   For Paula, Zach, Katelyn, Mum and Dad.
>   Many thanks to Mal Aubrey (GTA and all training organizations for their input.
>   To the De La Salle Brothers for their selfless work with all students.
>   Thanks also to Dr Pauline Carter for her unwavering support of all Maths teachers.
>   This is for all students who value learning, who are willing to work hard and who have character … and are characters!

Carole Vella:
>   For Richard and Mum.

The publisher would like to thank the many copyright holders who have kindly granted us permission to reproduce material throughout this text. Every effort has been made to contact all rights holders, but in the unlikely event that anything has been overlooked, please contact the publisher directly and we will happily make the necessary arrangements at the earliest opportunity.

ENGLISH

Unit 1: Speaking, Listening and Communication

Short-answer questions

Specific instructions to students

- These are exercises to help you to make relevant and extended contributions to discussions, allowing for and responding to others' input.
- They will also help you prepare for and contribute to the formal discussion of ideas and opinions, as well as help you to make different kinds of contribution to discussions and present information/points of view clearly and in appropriate language.
- Read the activities below, then answer accordingly.

Task 1 🕒

Question 1

Using this list of scenarios, with a partner, perform the role-play, giving and receiving instructions, explanations and descriptions.

a   A customer asks for directions to the nearest chemist.

b   The supermarket will be closing one hour early today for a thorough stock check. All staff are expected to stay and help with the stock check. They should report to their supervisor for details.

c   A customer takes a packet of cereal back to the customer service desk, complaining that when s/he opened the bag it was less than one quarter full. The customer wants a refund.

As you take part in each role-play, make sure you review your progress by using the review sheet below.

Skill	I can do this (✔ tick the box)	Where else would I use this skill in life, work?
Make relevant and extended contributions to discussions, allowing for and responding to others' input		
Prepare for and contribute to the formal discussion of ideas and opinions		
Make different kinds of contribution to discussions		
Present information/points of view clearly and in appropriate language		

Question 2

Conversation skills

Using a timer, hold a five-minute conversation with a partner about health and safety in a supermarket. After the five minutes, write in the box below how you feel the conversation went. Was it successful? What were the good points and what were the bad points?

Answer:

Unit 2: Spelling and Proofreading Skills

Short-answer questions

Specific instructions to students

- These are exercises to help you to identify and correct spelling errors.
- Read the activities below, then answer accordingly.

Task 1 🔲

Complaint about the Cinema

Read the following passage.

Dear Sir

I wish to complane about the flm I saw last night at your cinama. The **quality** of the pitcher was **terrible** and their were marks that kept appeering on the screen as if there was dirt on the projecter lense. To make things **worse**, all the way threw they're were people talking and laffing so loudly I couln't hear the words. Three times, mobile phones went of during the flm. I would like a **refund** of my tickit money wich was £5.50.

Yours faithfully

Gita Patel (Miss)

Question 1

Some of the words in the text are in **bold**. Look up these words in a dictionary and write the meanings below.

quality _____

worse _____

terrible _____

refund _____

Question 2

There are 16 spelling mistakes in the text above. Correct the words below.

complane .... projecter .... couln't ....

flm... lense... of...

cinama... threw .... flm...

pitcher .... they're .... tickit...

their .... laffing .... wich ....

appeering...

Task 2

The Local Shopping Centre

Read the following passage.

Alice and Darren go shopping at the local shopping centre. The shopping centre is very bussy as the retail outlats are having hugge sales. Over 300 shops are **located** there, and with late-night shoping, peope offen stay there for a meal. Alice and Darren both head for the clothing shops first to chek out the different desiner labels. They both like the jeans on sale but they don't have enugh money to buy a pair. Darren then sees some t-shirts that look trendy, and he has just enough to buy two of them. Alice wants to look at mobile phones, so they both head off to find the mobile phone store.

They locate the mobile phone stoure in the midle of the shopping centre, and inside there are two staff members standing around. Alice looks at the pre-paid phones while Darren looks at the range of mobile phone covars. Alice asks if she can see a top-of-the-range pre-paid phone. The staff mumber shows her the best one available, and **explains** that it comes free with their £49-per-month phone plan. By choosing this plan, she would get over £130 in credit each month but she would have to sighn up for 24 months. Alice thanks the staff member for the **advice** and walks over to Darren, who is now looking at the mobile phones on the other side of the shop. Darren is thinking of upgruding his mobile, but isn't sure if he can **afford** to do it as most of the newer mobiles would cost him a fair bit. Alice and Darren deside to leave it for now and go to grab a bite to eat as they are both getting hungray.

The food court is really busy, but they manage to find an empty table to sit down at. They look up at the menus above the food stands and narrow their choices down to the following: chicken nuggets with chips, chicken vindaloo, lasagnia, pork and vegetable curry, beef vindaloo, chilli con carne or a beefburger with chips. It is getting late so they quickly oarder and eat their meal before going to the music store. Alice and Darren both love musik and don't find it hard to spend money in the store. Both of them purchase two CDs each, which were on specal, with a 20% discount. It is now almost 9.00 p.m. so they decide to head over to the bus stasion and catch a bus home.

Question 1

Some of the words in the text are in **bold**. Look up these words in a dictionary and write the meanings below.

located _____

explains _____

advice _____

afford _____

Question 2

a Which shopping centre do Alice and Darren go to?

Answer:

_____

b Name one thing that Alice and Darren would like to buy.

Answer:

_____

c What is Darren thinking of doing?

Answer:

_____

d What do both Alice and Darren love and what do they both buy?

Answer:

_____

e How do Alice and Darren get home?

Answer:

_____

Question 3

There are 22 spelling mistakes in the text. Correct the words below. You may use a dictionary.

bussy	enugh	deside ....
outlats	stoure..................................	hungray ....
hugge	midle	lasagnia...............................
shoping	covars	oarder.................................
peope.................................	mumber	musik...................................
offen...................................	sighn...................................	specal..................................
chek	upgruding	stasion ....
desiner		

Task 3 ④

Spelling

The memo and instructions below contain a number of spelling mistakes. Read the texts, looking out for the spelling mistakes, then answer the questions.

Question 1

1 From: Sarah

2 To: Marta

3 Just a quick note to let you know that Paula

4 rang at 9.30am about the delivery of computers.

5 There has bean a hold up in the warehouse and

6 They cannot deliver the computers this week.

7 She cannot give you a definate date for delivery

8 Can you ring her after 12.30.

9 She is on 020 8765 9345.

a Which lines contain spelling mistakes?

Answer:

_____

b Now write the incorrect and correct versions of the words.

Answer:

_____

_____

Question 2

1   **FIRE SAFETY INSTRUCTIONS**

2   In the event of fire leave the building imediately

3   Do not stop to take any valuables.

4   Walk slowly and calmly to the Assembly Point

5   Remain there untill told to return to the building.

a Which lines contain spelling mistakes?

Answer:

_____

b Now write the incorrect and correct versions of the words.

Answer:

_____

_____

Task 4

Proofreading

Proofread the following personal statement to find the mistakes, then write it out again including all the correct words.

Personal statement for a job

I wood like to be considered for the job of Head Shop Assistance, has I have a lot of expereince in this field. I have worked in my local newsagent shop were I was responsible for serving customers, menning the till and occasionally supervising people. I have also worked on saturdays at Kendals as a sales assistance in the electrical department while I was doing my diploma at collage.

I am a very poliet indivijual with excellent intrpersonal skills, who is able to put costumers at easy. I am very trustworthy as I waz often asked to look after the till and too cash up at night time when I workt at Kendals. I am a very punctual individual who can be relyed on too be on time.

 I had also had experience of supervisin staff in a local shop when the owners went on holiday. I was able to make the shop run smoothy in their absence.

With all that I have disclose above, I would like you to consider me four the above post. I have the wright qualities and abilities to woUld appreciate the oportunity to develop my knowledge and skills further. I look forward to hear form you soon.

Answer:

Short-answer questions

Specific instructions to students

- The following questions will help you practise your grammar and punctuation.
- Read the following questions, then answer accordingly.

Task 1 (L1) (L2)

How to use Commas

We use commas in two main ways, to separate items in a list and to break up sentences into clauses to make the sentence easier to understand. Remember to use the word 'and' or 'or' before the last item in a list, and don't use a comma before those words.

QUESTION 1

Rewrite these sentences, adding and/or, commas and full stops where needed.

a Deepak has cereal tea orange juice toast for breakfast

Answer:

_____

_____

b I go to work on Mondays Wednesdays Thursdays Fridays

Answer:

_____

_____

c Wendy chose skirts tops and dresses for the customer

Answer:

_____

d Julie orders pens paper pencils fax paper printer paper marker pens

Answer:

_____

_____

e Mark telephones suppliers customers on a daily basis

Answer:

_____

f Dewsbury has shops bars cafes lots of pubs

Answer:

_____

QUESTION 2

Complete these sentences by adding commas.

a Despite me asking her not to Kate Lindley my manager sent the letter.

Answer:

_____

_____

b Although it was raining we went for lunch in the cafe.

Answer:

_____

c The employee the one who started at Christmas has now left.

Answer:

_____

d Eventually I found the missing printer cartridge.

Answer:

_____

e Jenny my colleague with brown hair lives next door.

Answer:

_____

f   In the end even though I had a headache I went on the staff outing.

Answer:

_____

_____

Task 2 🔟

Conjunctions

Conjunctions are linking words that we can use to join up two sentences. Examples of conjunctions are: because, although, as, or, so.

QUESTION 1

Insert a conjunction into the spaces to complete each sentence.

a   My name is David .... I am a shelf-stacker.

Answer:

_____

b   I live in Wolverhampton now, ... I was born in Wales.

Answer:

_____

_____

c   I am in the warehouse today unloading stock .... my colleague James is off sick.

Answer:

_____

_____

d   I want to pass my functional level 1 English .... I must work hard in class.

Answer:

_____

_____

e   I am very tired today .... it was the staff Christmas party last night.

Answer:

_____

_____

Over to you!

Write five sentences about what you do at work or at college. Make sure you use conjunctions, and try to use different ones to the examples above.

_____

_____

_____

_____

_____

_____

_____

_____

_____

_____

_____

_____

_____

Task 3

QUESTION 1

Which linking word or phrase could you use instead of 'whereas'?

Answer:

QUESTION 2

What does the linking word 'alternatively' mean?

Answer:

QUESTION 3

What punctuation is missing from the following sentence?

the retail industry has undergone many changes since 1980 and the number of people employed in the industry has trebled to almost 2.7 million people in that time almost 11% of all those employed. the industry is now the second largest employer in the UK.

Answer:

QUESTION 4

What is wrong with the following text? Correct the following sentences.

PC World is part of the Dixons Group (DSG International), which has more than 1,400 stores worldwide in countries including the uk, ireland, scandinavia, france, spain and the czech republic. It trades under a number of names including currys, pc world and the link in the uk and ireland. In other countries it is variously known as pc city, uniEuro, electro world and kotsovolos.

Answer:

QUESTION 5

What is wrong with the following text?

Why not apply for a Business Retail Apprenticeship at Balham College? Youll be able to gain excellent Customer Service skills as well as many other capabilities. To find out more, call Balham College reception on 01435 778367.

Answer:

QUESTION 6

Can you identify the mistake in this job application letter?

Dear Madam

I wish to apply for the vacancy of shop assistant at your Gloucester shop, as advertised in this week's Gloucester Globe.

I have just completed my Level 2 Business Retail Diploma coarse at Dinsdale Park College and am now looking for work in the Gloucester area.

I enclose a copy of my CV and look forward to hearing from you.

Yours faithfully

Matthew Morris

Answer:

QUESTION 7

a   Rewrite the following paragraph and add the missing full stops, commas and capital letters to this text telling you about stock control.

Stock control

for any business, stock represents money which has been invested until the stock is sold this money cannot be earned unsold stock can lose value, therefore retailers need to sell as soon as possible having too much stock is a poor investment and having too little stock means poor service to the customer it is obviously necessary to get the balance right a good system of stock control is vital if the business is to maximise profitability as well as controlling the level of stock it is important to keep the stock in good condition by optimising storage conditions.

Answer:

QUESTION 8

Add commas to the following text to make the sense clearer.

> **Advertising in a retail business**
>
> There are many different types of advertising in retail which include: television radio newspapers magazines cinema billboards posters direct mail internet and market research. The timing of advertising can be seasonal or for a new product which in turn builds customer loyalty and improves customer product and customer service.

Answer:

Task 4

Grammar quiz

QUESTION 1

What is grammar?

(1) Punctuation, e.g. full stops and capital letters.

(2) Correct use of words and sentence structure.

(3) Spellings.

Answer:

QUESTION 2

Which of these sentences is wrong and why?

(1) I must of forgotten it.

(2) He must have gone into town.

(3) She should've taken her umbrella.

Answer:

QUESTION 3

Which of these sentences is wrong and why?

(1) We were waiting for a taxi.

(2) He was running down the street.

(3) We was in the queue for ages.

Answer:

QUESTION 4

What is meant by 'parts of speech'?

(1) Your mouth, tongue and lungs.

(2) Types of words such as nouns, verbs and adjectives.

Answer:

QUESTION 5

What does 'literally' mean? Put it in a sentence so that it is grammatically correct.

Answer:

QUESTION 6

Their, *there* and *they're* are homophones. Which one should be used in the following sentence?

….. is a small town far away.

Answer:

Short-answer questions

Specific instructions to students

- This is an exercise to help you understand what you read.
- Read the following activity, then answer the questions that follow.

Comprehension Task

Read the following passage and answer the questions in sentence form.

The students had a day off from college so they decided to go to the local shopping centre. David was the only one who had passed his driving test so he was the driver. The students got into the car and they all made their way to the shopping centre. When they arrived there they all piled out of the car and went to the food court. They were all hungry as no one had had breakfast, and it was already 10.00 a.m. Ian bought a chocolate milkshake for £2.80, Bruce bought a beefburger meal deal which included a drink for £4.95, Julie bought a doughnut and an ice cream for £3.95 and David had a piece of cheesecake for £3.95. They all sat down and ate before Ian and Bruce headed off to look at the bicycle shop. Ian had had his bike stolen two weeks earlier, so he was in the market for a new one.

David and Julie went into the jeans shop first, to have a look at the newest jeans that had come in. Julie tried on a pair of jeans before buying them, but David didn't end up buying anything. After that, David and Julie headed to the shoe shop where David bought a new pair of trainers for £59.99.

They all met up again outside the cinema as they were keen to see a film. It was Cheap Tuesday, so all the tickets only cost £10 for any film. David, Ian and Bruce all bought the popcorn and drink deal that cost £9.90 each. Julie only wanted a drink and this cost her £3.50. They all walked to Cinema 3 where the film was screening and sat in the back row. The start time for the film was 2.00 p.m. and it finished at 3.55 p.m. After the film they all went back to David's place and stayed there until 6.00 p.m. before heading home.

QUESTION 1

Who drove to the shopping centre and why?

Answer:

QUESTION 2

How much money did all four spend in total at the food court?

Answer:

QUESTION 3

Why did Ian want to look in the bicycle shop?

Answer:

QUESTION 4

How much did all four spend in total at the cinema?

Answer:

QUESTION 5

How long did the group spend at the shopping centre? State your answer in hours and minutes.

Answer:

Comprehension Task 2

Specific instructions to students

This is an exercise to help you understand what you read.

Read the following passage and answer the questions in sentence form.

The Key to Customer Satisfaction

The key to most businesses' success in Retail is customer satisfaction. Giving customers everything they expect and MORE makes customers return. The best way to hold on to customers is to provide friendly service and accurate information, and constantly add more and more value to your products and services.

In order to improve your customer service department you need to ask new questions to improve your services. As well as this you need to review your company customer care policies and continually ask how to improve customer satisfaction, so that you can stay competitive in these changing times.

By keeping your customers happy, your business will grow and improve.

QUESTION 1

What is the key to business success?

Answer:

QUESTION 2

What type of information needs to be provided to customers?

Answer:

QUESTION 3

What needs to be reviewed?

Answer:

QUESTION 4

What happens when you keep your clients happy?

Answer:

Comprehension Task 3

The advert below was pinned on the staff notice board. Look at the advert then answer the questions.

LEE PARK
FIREWORKS DISPLAY

Saturday 5th November
18.00 to 21.00

Fascinating fireworks and fantastic food

Every employee and family welcome.

**Limited tickets available.
Don't delay, book today!**

Lighting of the bonfire	18.30
Childrens' face painting and crafts	18.00 – 19.00
Food served	19.00 – 20.00
Fireworks	20.00 – 21.00

QUESTION 1

Where will the fireworks display take place?

Answer:

_____

QUESTION 2

Name three things happening at this event.

Answer:

_____

_____

_____

QUESTION 3

This text is an advert. What are adverts designed to do? Tick the correct boxes:

a describe ☐   c persuade ☐

b inform ☐   d instruct ☐

QUESTION 4

Name three of the features used in this text.

Answer:

_____

_____

_____

QUESTION 5

The times in the text are in 24-hour format. Write the times again below in 12-hour format.

18:00 _____

18:30 _____

19:00 _____

20:00 _____

21:00 _____

QUESTION 6

What time will food be served?

Answer:

_____

QUESTION 7

The date on the text is written in the long form. Write the date again below in short form.

Answer:

_____

QUESTION 8

How long will the display last?

Answer:

_____

Unit 5: Homophones

Short-answer questions

Specific instructions to students

- The following questions relate to words that sound the same, but are spelt differently and have different meanings. These words are known as homophones.
- Read the questions carefully, then answer accordingly.

QUESTION 1

The following sentences are about two shop assistants that have decided to go on holiday together.

a Check your knowledge of *there, their* and *they're* in the following sentences. Only one sentence is correct. Which one is it?

(1) They're are too many training courses booked while there away so they will have to be cancelled.

(2) The manager realized that there holiday will be taken the same time as two others.

(3) They're going on their holiday in the early hours of Friday morning.

(4) There going to be short staffed all week so some staff may need to do overtime.

Answer:

_____

_____

b Check your knowledge of *where, were* and *we're* in the following sentences. Only one sentence is correct. Which one is it?

(1) When we get to our destination, we're not sure were we'll go first.

(2) We're sure we'll be fine, when we know where we're going.

(3) If there's a delay, where sure that we're going to miss our connecting flight.

(4) Once we find the hotel, were going to shower and change and go straight out.

Answer:

_____

_____

c Check your knowledge of *too, to* and *two* in the following sentences. Only one sentence is correct. Which one is it?

(1) The two of us are going to go on holiday to New York too.

(2) We want to go too Staten Island too.

(3) We're concerned that there'll be two many people on the Metro in New York.

(4) To get too Staten Island, the two of us will need to catch the ferry.

Answer:

_____

_____

d Check your knowledge of *buy, by* and *bye* in the following sentences. Only one sentence is correct. Which one is it?

(1) We'll each have to bye a ticket to get to Staten Island by ferry.

(2) By the way, we'll have to make sure that we buy plenty of souvenirs to take home.

(3) Buy the time we get home, it will be a struggle to say bye to each other.

(4) By all accounts, we'll have to bye some waterproofs for the ferry journey.

Answer:

_____

_____

e Check your knowledge of *pause, paws* and *pours* in the following sentences. Only one sentence is correct. Which one is it?

  (1) If it paws down with rain, we'll go to Central Park Zoo.

  (2) If there's a pause in the rain, we'll go and see the polar bears.

  (3) It doesn't matter if their pours get wet, as they'll be swimming in their pool anyway.

  (4) Once it starts raining, though, it just paws and paws.

Answer:

_____

_____

f Check your knowledge of *heal, he'll* and *heel* in the following sentences. Only one sentence is correct. Which one is it?

  (1) While running in the rain, I slipped and fell on my knee and broke the heal of my shoe.

  (2) My knee is really sore and bruised, so it will take a couple of days to heel.

  (3) I'm so glad that Andrew is with me, as he'll have to lend me a bit of support.

  (4) I couldn't find a cobbler, so I'll have to wait to get my heal fixed when I get home.

Answer:

_____

_____

QUESTION 2

Check your knowledge of *there, their* and *they're* in the following sentences. Read each sentence and write the correct word in the space provided, from the words provided below:

there   their   they're

a The deli counter assistant in the supermarket was busy sorting _____ salami and ham orders.

b _____ was just enough seating in the 'Employee of the Month' presentation.

c I wonder if that is the personal shopper over _____?

d I asked the receptionist to welcome the Regional Retail Managers and to hang up _____ coats for them.

e It's nearly 11.00 a.m. and _____ going to be here in a minute.

f There are some new ranges of colours in stock; I've heard that _____ really good?

g I believe that the wholesalers have got all of _____ new colour shades in stock.

h I'll have to go to the wholesalers again, I was only _____ last week.

i I must leave work on time to get to the wholesalers before _____ closed.

QUESTION 3

Check your knowledge of *where, were* and *we're* in the following sentences. Read each sentence and write the correct word in the space provided, from the words provided below:

where   were   we're

a We always have our market stall _____ we know that we will attract plenty of customers.

b _____ always making sure that all butchering knives are clean and sterilized before use.

c If the knives aren't sterilized, _____ not prepared to use them due to the risk of cross-infection.

d When setting out stock, we always have everything laid out _____ it is in easy reach of the warehouse pickers.

e When cutting material, _____ always checking that each length of fabric is level to match the next.

f We make sure that any sewing alterations are always carried out _____ there is good light.

g We make sure that the customer has plenty of time to choose from the swatches of material and tend to leave them in view _____ they can refer to them during the curtain consultation.

h We always make sure that the post is damage free before it leaves the sorting office; there's nothing worse than if the customer _____ to complain about the postal service.

i If we _____ not to offer any aftercare advice as part of the service when a customer purchases a computer, we would be providing a disservice to our customers.

j _____ always happy when a customer recommends our services as a personal shopper, as it makes us feel satisfied with the service we've given.

QUESTION 4

The following chart relates to words that sound the same, but are spelt differently and have different meanings (homophones). Complete the chart, where applicable, providing clues for the word's meaning and / or a short sentence to put the word in the correct context.

Words	Clues for meaning	Short sentence
Hear	To listen to.	
Here	In this spot.	
Weak		I felt so weak this morning, I could hardly move.
Week	A period of 7 consecutive days.	
Piece		I'll only have a small piece of chocolate cake, thank you.
Peace	Freedom from strife, arguments or war.	
Cue		During the play, he spotted his cue to speak.
Queue	To form a line while waiting.	
Allowed		
Aloud		You're not meant to speak aloud in a library.
Knew	The past tense of 'know'.	
New		

Stationery	Writing materials such as pens, pencils, paper and envelopes.	
Stationary		Locking the castors on a stool makes it stationary.
Whole	The complete sum, amount or quantity of anything.	
Hole		I must have lost my money through the hole in my pocket.
Draught	A current of air, usually of a different temperature, entering an enclosed space.	
Draft	A first sketch, or version, of writing, which could be subject to revision.	
Draw		
Drawer	A lidless container that slides in and out of a chest or table.	

QUESTION 5

Which of these pairs of words are NOT homophones?

(1) hear / here

(2) write / right

(3) stop / cease

(4) new / knew

Answer:

_____

Short-answer questions

Specific instructions to students

- The following questions relate to writing letters and emails.
- Read the questions carefully, then answer accordingly.

Task 1

QUESTION 1

Which type of writing is likely to be informal in style?

(1) Making an appointment to see the bank manager

(2) Confirming an interview date

(3) Email to a friend

(4) Making a complaint

Answer:

QUESTION 2

As well as thinking about the recipient of your letter or email, what else do you need to think about when writing a letter or email?

(1) The content

(2) The style

(3) The layout

(4) All of the above

Answer:

QUESTION 3

True or false? When writing an email, you need to select the email address of the person you want to receive it before selecting the 'send' button.

Answer:

QUESTION 4

How would you describe the 'content' of a letter or email?

(1) The formality with which you are writing

(2) The ideas and information you are writing

(3) The amount of text you are writing

Answer:

QUESTION 5

When sending an email, if you want other people to receive it but do not want to share their email addresses, which box would you select?

(1) 'Forward'

(2) 'Cc'

(3) 'Bcc'

(4) 'Send/Receive'

Answer:

Task 2

QUESTION 1

Parts a) to h) relate to this letter of complaint. Please read it carefully and refer to it to answer the questions.

Booths Department Store

37 North Street

Millwharf

Ipswich

PE48 7ER

9 April 2012

The Manager

Total Photocopying Equipment for the 21st Century

Fenchurch Street

Leeds

LS17 3QQ

Dear Sir or Madam

1   Your office contacted me on 15 March regarding the urgent repairs that were required to the office

2   photocopier model HPT35902 which had been identified as representing a fire hazard. Your company

3   service engineer carried out the neccessary repairs on 29 March.

4   Within a day I noticed that the paper was scoring hot and jamming each time a document needed

5   photocopying, so I cannot run the risk of using this piece of equipment. This has had a knock-on effect

6   of not being able to keep our promise to customers that we deal with any complaints regarding stock

7   bought from our shop within seven days. As you can appreciate, we need to keep a copy of each

8   complaint and cannot do so due to the fault with the photocopier.

9   Myself and my colleagues rely heavily on the use of this photocopier and the loss of it has caused

10   us great inconvenience and is giving our store a bad reputation. As none of this is our fault, I am

11   appealing to you to replace the photocopier and to reimburse the company for the loss of earnings

12   which it has incurred.

Yours sincerely

Bethany Lewis

Administrative Assistant

a What is wrong with the closing phrase at the end of the letter?

Answer:

_____

_____

b What does the word 'inconvenience' mean, in Line 10?

Answer:

_____

c Which paragraph of the letter outlines the reason for the complaint?

Answer:

_____

d Line 4 contains a spelling error. What is the word and how should it be spelt?

Answer:

_____

e Which word or phrase, used in the letter, means 'to pay me back'?

Answer:

_____

f What is the main complaint in this letter?

Answer:

_____

_____

g How would you describe the style of writing used by Bethany in her letter?

Answer:

_____

h The paragraph of Bethany's letter in which she uses her most persuasive language is?

Answer:

_____

QUESTION 2

Formal and informal letters

Read the following letters and compare the differences.

Informal (slang) version

> Hi
>
> Heard about the job, reckon I would be great at it! I've done that kind of work before, working in my local and fink shop is buzzing. They even trusted me with the readies, like. I was a cleaner before that, but that was gross and I don't wanna do that again! Give us a chance, ring me on 01709 245 6789. Cheers!
>
> Sam

Formal version

> Dear Sir / Madam,
>
> I am writing to express my interest in the stock controller's vacancy.
>
> I have experience of working in a shop where I was responsible for handling money and operating the till. I enjoy working in a busy atmosphere, have great people skills, and can work under pressure. I have previously worked as a cleaner, and could apply this experience to keeping the bar in a good and hygienic condition.
>
> I look forward to hearing from you.
> Please contact me on 01709 245 6789.
>
> Yours faithfully
>
>
> Sam Goodwin

Comparison of differences between both letters

Answer:

c I have got responsibilities with regard to Health and Safety, and I will need to be trained.

Answer:

_____

_____

d I should not need much help for problems that arise at work as I have a staff handbook.

Answer:

_____

_____

e It is only 10.30 a.m. and I cannot believe how hungry I am!

Answer:

_____

_____

f He won't believe that I missed the last bus home after the work party.

Answer:

_____

_____

g She doesn't like to be absent from work as it puts too much pressure on other members of staff.

Answer:

_____

_____

Task 3 ⓛ⓵ ⓛ⓶

QUESTION 1

The following exercises contain a mixture of sentences that have either already been shortened, using apostrophes, or require shortening. Read them carefully, and then reword the sentence accordingly.

a Retail assistants should understand that they have got rights in the workplace.

Answer:

_____

_____

b He should have respected the rights of other members of staff in the workplace.

Answer:

_____

_____

QUESTION 2

If you are applying for a job, what do you not need to include?

(1) What qualifications and experience you have

(2) Your plans for the future

(3) How long it will take to commute

(4) Why you want to work for the company

Answer:

_____

_____

QUESTION 3

Caroline has written in response to the advertisement that she spotted in the Wigan Daily Post, shown below.

> Till Operator required for local supermarket.
>
> Must have 1 year's experience.
>
> Please send your CV and covering letter, to:
>
> Paul Smith
>
> Bettavalue Supermarket
>
> 27 Bold Street
>
> Wigan

She has asked you to look over her covering letter to see if she has included all the relevant points, before she posts it. She has also asked if you can help her write it again, if necessary.

> Hi there
>
> I want the job you've put in the local news paper this week. I've been in retail for 2 years and I can get people to vouch for me, if you want. Here's a list of my qualifications and where I've worked before, in with this letter.
>
> You can call me on 07562 725094
>
> Caroline

Help Caroline by rewriting the short covering letter to accompany her CV including the correct structure, content and layout for a formal cover letter.

Answer:

Task 4

The Administration Manager at Morestores Ltd has dropped a memo into your in-tray asking you to complete a purchase order for computer supplies that she needs urgently (she assumes you have a price list). The items are as follows: cordless mouse, ergonomic keyboard, HP deskjet cartridge – black for a 690C ink jet printer, HP laserjet 5000 toner, mouse mat, wrist rest, screen clean wipes, aerosol duster for cleaning keyboards, foot rest and computer VDU filter.

Complete the purchase order.

PURCHASE ORDER

DATE:

PURCHASE ORDER:

CUSTOMER ID:

SHIP TO:

Morestores Ltd
33 Mill Lane
Wigan

ITEM	AMOUNT

SUBTOTAL TO INCLUDE TAX

	SUBTOTAL
	TAX
	S&H
	OTHER
	TOTAL DUE

OTHER COMMENTS

1. Total payment due in 10 days

If you have any questions about this purchase order, please contact the Administration Assistant.

Task 5

Leaving Gift

A colleague (Jack Smith) at work is retiring. You have been asked to organize a collection for a leaving gift and get people to sign a card. Write an email to your workmates to let them know about this. You should mention:

- who is retiring

- why you are sending the email

- how people can give money and by when

- how they can sign the card

Spending five minutes, write a rough draft in the box below. When writing, keep the following things in mind:

- purpose

- audience

- content

- tone

Check your work carefully, use a dictionary if you need to.

Draft:

Now take ten minutes to write your final email.

Final email:

The collection for your colleague has raised £90.00. Using an online website or catalogue, choose a suitable gift for him. He enjoys gardening, DIY and likes gadgets.

Make a note of the gift here:

_____

Write another email to your workmates letting them know what you have done. You should include:

- thanks for their contributions

- how much was raised

- what gift you have chosen

- when the presentation will be made

Answer:

Now check your work. For level 1 check for correct use of capital letters and full stops, proper sentences, spelling and grammar, and use of paragraphs. For level 2 check for correct use of capital letters, proper sentences, commas and apostrophes, spelling and grammar, use of paragraphs and logical order.

Task 6 L2

QUESTION 1

You are a Business Retail student at Lowham College and you have volunteered to help with organizing the college's annual fashion show. In order for you to help out, Bob Moore, Head of Fashion has asked you first to read the following four pieces of communication:

a A letter from a charity director to the college fashion department.

Moulton Street Shelter
14 Moulton Street
Lowham
LW4 8XY

Bob Moore
Head of Fashion
Dept of Creative Industries
Lowham College
Old Hill
Lowham
LW7 1CV

14th July 2013

Dear Mr Moore

I'm writing on behalf of Moulton Street Shelter, a local charity of which I am a director.

Our volunteers help run temporary accommodation for homeless people, and we're well known for the evening soup kitchen that we run during the winter months.

As a charity we're always looking for innovative ways to raise money in order to continue our work. I'm aware that the college currently has some particularly talented students in the fashion department and an excellent Business Retail Department. I wondered if you would be interested in helping to organize a fashion show? This would involve organizing samples of student work, volunteer models (from willing students!) and generally helping out with the event.

I have a couple of possible venues in mind. Layton Hall Hotel has a suitable event room with a large stage that could be used as a catwalk, and The Seven Stars at Thorpe Street has a surprisingly large function room, although there is no stage. We're hoping that one of these venues will support the event by reducing or waiving the rental fee.

I do understand if you feel that you can't spare sufficient time to help us. However, the benefits are sure to outweigh the effort involved. It would be excellent publicity for your departments and for the college in general, as well as being a tremendous showcase for your talented students. Most of all it would help to support our work with the homeless. In anticipation of a positive response, I would like to give you a call next week to discuss the next steps.

Yours sincerely

Sophie Saunders

---

b   An advert for a function room at a local hotel.

Layton Hall Hotel
The Event Room

Layton Hall Hotel's Event Room is available for hire from 8 am – midnight, seven days a week. With its clean, contemporary décor, the Event Room is suitable for a variety of events and has limitless opportunities for you to be creative with the surroundings. Luxury washrooms are close by and free Wi-Fi is available throughout.

Comprising 45-square-metres plus stage, the Event Room can comfortably seat 150 dinner-style, or up to 220 theatre-style with a stage. Fully air-conditioned and with an array of stage lighting, the Event Room is the first choice in Lowham for any kind of musical, theatrical or stage-based performance.

Layton Hall Hotel is three miles from the centre of Lowham and we have ample free parking.

The Event Room is available on an hourly rate of £25 per hour; a daily rate (8 am – 5 pm) of £195; or an evening rate (6 pm – midnight) of £125.

To discuss your forthcoming event at Layton Hall Hotel,
please call the Booking Manager on 01234 77665
or email bookings@laytonhh.biz

c   An advert for an inn/hotel.

The Seven Stars – *tradition, comfort and hospitality in the heart of Lowham*

Dating back to the 17th century, the former coaching house of The Seven Stars combines traditional atmosphere with modern comfort in the heart of the market town of Lowham. Why not enjoy lunch in our panelled bar, or in the comfortable Bowery Restaurant, open from 11.30am to 2.30pm? Evening meals are served daily from 6–9pm.

Need accommodation? The Seven Stars also boasts five comfortable double rooms, all en-suite with satellite TV channels, direct dial telephones and tea/coffee-making facilities. Every room has sweeping views over Lowham town centre. Available from £25 per person per night.

Do you require a room for a wedding or event? Our spacious function room is available for hire and can comfortably seat up to 200 for parties etc. With rates from £65 for an evening, why look anywhere else?

Please note that The Seven Stars has limited free car parking. However, Lowham Central public car park is a mere 50 metres away (hourly rates).

d An email from the head of the fashion department to the charity director.

To: s.saunders@moultonshelter.biz

Cc:

Subject: *Fashion Show*

Dear Sophie

It was really good to meet you last Tuesday. I must say that I'm very excited about this fashion show, and our students are really pleased to have this opportunity to present their work to the public, as well as support Moulton Street Shelter.

Further to your request for details, I'm pleased to tell you that seven students (five female, two male) have so far confirmed that they will model on the night. We already have four fashion students working on a 'collection' for modelling, and they will all have items for sale on the night:

– Ali Smith: specialises in women's clothing

– Jack Williams: hand-printed unisex t-shirts and hoodies

– Rasme Dulal: colourful one-off women's bags, made from recycled fabrics

– Carrie-Anne Skinner: evening wear for young women (prom dresses, etc).

As requested I've investigated the two venues for suitability. The function room at The Seven Stars is, how shall I say, very 'traditional', and while it's certainly spacious enough for us to place the seating down either side of a 'catwalk' aisle, the décor is a bit out of keeping with a contemporary fashion show. The staff are friendly though and they agreed to give us the room for free. On the other hand, the Event Room at Layton Hall Hotel is superb, with a really modern feel to it, and it has a stage. They've agreed to reduce the hire fee to just £50. What do you think?

We'll also need to talk about the next steps in publicizing the show. Any ideas?

Looking forward to meeting up again soon,

Bob Moore

Bob Moore
Head of Fashion
Department of Creative Industries
Lowham College

Your task now is to email Layton Hall Hotel to book the Event Room. Using the template overleaf, your email should include:

• full details of the event itself and what seating layout is required

• the date and the time (Wednesday October 3rd, from 6pm until 10pm)

• a reminder that they've agreed to reduce the hire fee as the purpose is to raise funds for charity

Write your email here:

To:
Cc:
Subject:

QUESTION 2

The local newspaper is interested in the charity fashion show and has invited someone from the college to write an article. Bob Moore has asked you to write an informative article about the forthcoming show, including details of the cost (£5 for adults, £3 for students), the confirmed designers and also the charity that will benefit from the event. The article should also be persuasive, as you want as many of the public to attend as possible.

Answer:

MATHEMATICS

It is important to show your workings out to indicate how you calculated your answer. Use this book to practise the questions and record your answers. Use extra paper if necessary to record your workings out.

Unit 7: General Mathematics

Short-answer questions

Specific instructions to students

- This unit will help you to improve your general mathematical skills.
- Read the following questions and answer all of them in the spaces provided.
- You need to show all working, you can use the blank Notes pages at the back of this book.

QUESTION 1

What unit of measurement would you use to measure:

a   the size of a person's waistline for fitting jeans?

Answer:

_____

b   the temperature of an oven in a patisserie?

Answer:

_____

c   the change given from a pound coin?

Answer:

_____

d   the weight of a jumper?

Answer:

_____

e   the speed of a delivery truck?

Answer:

_____

f   the height of a retail shop?

Answer:

_____

g   the weight of a fridge?

Answer:

_____

QUESTION 2

Write an example of each of the following and give an instance where it may be found in the retail industry.

a   Percentages

Answer:

_____

b   Decimals

Answer:

_____

_____

c   Fractions

Answer:

_____

_____

d   Mixed numbers

Answer:

_____

_____

e   Ratios

Answer:

_____

_____

f   Angles

Answer:

_____

QUESTION 3
Convert the following units:

a   12 kg to g

Answer:

_____

b   4 tonnes to kilograms

Answer:

_____

c   120 cm to m

Answer:

_____

d   1140 millitres to litres

Answer:

_____

e   1650 g to kg

Answer:

_____

f   1880 kg to tonnes

Answer:

_____

g   13 m to centimetres

Answer:

_____

h   4.5 litres to millitres

Answer:

_____

QUESTION 4
Write the following in descending order:

0.4   0.04   4.1   40.0   400.00   4.0

Answer:

_____

QUESTION 5
Write the decimal number that goes between the following:

a   0.2 and 0.4

Answer:

_____

b   1.8 and 1.9

Answer:

_____

c   12.4 and 12.6

Answer:

_____

d   28.3 and 28.4

Answer:

_____

e   101.5 and 101.7

Answer:

_____

QUESTION 6
Round off the following numbers to two decimal places:

a   12.346

Answer:

_____

b   2.251

Answer:

_____

c   123.897

Answer:

_____

d   688.882

Answer:

_____

e   1209.741

Answer:

_____

QUESTION 7

Calculate the following to the nearest whole number:

a $1288 \times 19 =$

Answer:

b $201 \times 20 =$

Answer:

c $497 \times 12.2 =$

Answer:

d $1008 \times 10.3 =$

Answer:

e $399 \times 22 =$

Answer:

f $201 - 19 =$

Answer:

g $502 - 61 =$

Answer:

h $1003 - 49 =$

Answer:

i $10\,001 - 199 =$

Answer:

j $99.99 - 39.8 =$

Answer:

QUESTION 8

What do the following add up to?

a   £4, £4.99 and £144.95

Answer:

b   £8.75, £6.90 and £312.55

Answer:

c   65 ml, 18 ml and 209 ml

Answer:

d   21.3 g, 119 g and 884.65 g

Answer:

QUESTION 9

Subtract the following:

a   2338 from 7117

Answer:

b   1786 from 3112

Answer:

c   5979 from 8014

Answer:

d   11 989 from 26 221

Answer:

e   108 767 from 231 111

Answer:

QUESTION 10

Use division to solve the following:

a 2177 divided by 7

Answer:

b $4484 \div 4 =$

Answer:

c 63.9 divided by 0.3

Answer:

d $121.63 \div 1.2 =$

Answer:

e $466.88 \div 0.8 =$

Answer:

The following information will help you answer Question 11.

To solve using BODMAS, in order from left to right solve the Brackets first, then Order ('to the power of'), then Division, then Multiplication, then Addition and lastly Subtraction. The following example has been done for your reference.

EXAMPLE :

Solve $(4 \times 7) \times 2 + 6 - 4$.

STEP 1

Solve the Brackets first: $(4 \times 7) = 28$

STEP 2

No Division so next solve Multiplication: $28 \times 2 = 56$

STEP 3

Addition is next: $56 + 6 = 62$

STEP 4

Subtraction is the last process: $62 - 4 = 58$

FINAL ANSWER
58

QUESTION 11

Using BODMAS solve:

a $(6 \times 9) \times 5 + 7 - 2$

Answer:

b $(9 \times 8) \times 4 + 6 - 1$

Answer:

c $3 \times (5 \times 7) + 11 - 8$

Answer:

d $6 + 9 - 5 \times (8 \times 3)$

Answer:

e $9 - 7 + 6 \times 3 + (9 \times 6)$

Answer:

f $(4 \times 3) - 6 + 9 \times 4 + (6 \times 7)$

Answer:

g $(4 \times 9) - (3 \times 7) + 16 - 11 \times 2$

Answer:

h $9 - 4 \times 6 + (6 \times 7) + (8 \times 9) - 23$

Answer:

Section A: Addition

Short-answer questions

Specific instructions to students

- This section will help you to improve your addition skills for basic operations.
- Read the questions below and answer all of them in the spaces provided.
- You need to show all working, you can use the blank Notes pages at the back of this book.

QUESTION 1

A shopper buys 200 g of ham, 150 g of salami and 270 g of turkey. How many grams is that in total?

Answer:

_____

QUESTION 2

A launderette worker buys packets of washing powder in three different sizes: 1.5 kg, 2.5 kg and 15 kg. How many kilograms of washing powder has he purchased in total?

Answer:

_____

QUESTION 3

A jewellery store stocks 327 rings, 368 bracelets and 723 various other pieces of fine jewellery. How many pieces does it stock in total?

Answer:

_____

QUESTION 4

A delivery van is driven 352 miles, 459 miles, 872 miles and 198 miles over 4 consecutive weeks. How far has the van been driven in total?

Answer:

_____

QUESTION 5

A furniture delivery van uses the following amounts of diesel over a month: 35.5 litres in week one, 42.9 litres in week two, 86.9 litres in week 3 and 66.2 litres in week four.

a How many litres were used in total?

Answer:

_____

b If diesel costs £1.40 per litre, how much was spent on fuel for the month?

Answer:

_____

QUESTION 6

A shopper buys a frying pan for £82.50, 4 chopping knives for £116.80 and a mixing bowl for £6.75, how much has been spent?

Answer:

_____

QUESTION 7

A cook buys 10 kg of mince and divides it into three containers of 2.6 kg, 3.2 kg and 1.8 kg. How many kg have been used?

Answer:

_____

QUESTION 8

A shopper buys a new electric cooker for £225.80, a chopping block for £26.99 and a set of knives for £88.50. How much has been spent in total?

Answer:

_____

QUESTION 9

A worker travels 36 miles, 33 miles, 37 miles and 44 miles over four weeks to get to and from the shopping centre where she works. How far has she travelled in total?

Answer:

_____

QUESTION 10

175 g, 180 g and 100 g of bacon are purchased to make different meals in a cafe. How much bacon was purchased in total?

Answer:

_____

Section B: Subtraction

Short-answer questions

Specific instructions to students

- This section will help you to improve your subtraction skills for basic operations.
- Read the following questions and answer all of them in the spaces provided.
- You need to show all working, you can use the blank Notes pages at the back of this book.

QUESTION 1

A shopper buys a 10 litre can of virgin olive oil. He uses 1.2 litres for cooking on one night, 1.7 litres on the next night and 1.1 litres on the third night.

a   How much oil is used in total?

Answer:

_____

b   How much oil is left in the can?

Answer:

_____

QUESTION 2

If one person uses 151 g of flour to make a cake and another person uses 169 g to make another, how much more flour has the first person used than the second?

Answer:

_____

QUESTION 3

A worker earns £650 per week. He spends £24.80 on food and £94.70 on petrol. How much is left?

Answer:

_____

QUESTION 4

A jeweller sells 39 bracelets from a box that contains 200 bracelets. How many are left?

Answer:

_____

QUESTION 5

The total bill for skate gear comes to £154.65. The manager takes off a discount of £15. How much does the bill now total?

Answer:

_____

QUESTION 6

Over the course of a year, a store manager drives 11 297 miles. Of this, 1835 miles was for her personal use, while the rest was for work. How far did she drive for work-related purposes?

Answer:

QUESTION 7

A delivery truck uses the following amounts of diesel over 3 months:

Month 1 – 225 litres

Month 2 – 313 litres

Month 3 – 296 litres

a How much diesel is used?

Answer:

b 1000 litres is budgeted for the 3 months. How much is left?

Answer:

QUESTION 8

During one month, a worker budgets to spend £34 on bus tickets. When he goes to purchase the tickets in bulk, he hands over a £50 note. How much change will he get?

Answer:

QUESTION 9

The yearly rental on a small shop comes to £24 231. The parents of a young owner help by putting £3,500 into the business to assist with the rent. How much more needs to be paid?

Answer:

QUESTION 10

A barista uses the following amounts of milk in three cups of hot beverages: 57 ml, 69 ml and 53 ml. If there were 2 litres of milk to begin with, how much would be left?

Answer:

Section C: Multiplication

Short-answer questions

Specific instructions to students

- This section will help you to improve your multiplication skills for basic operations.
- Read the following questions and answer all of them in the spaces provided.
- You need to show all working, you can use the blank Notes pages at the back of this book.

QUESTION 1

If a dry-cleaning van travels at 60 mph, how far will it travel in 6 hours?

Answer:

QUESTION 2

If a clothing delivery van travels at 80 mph, how far will it travel in 8 hours?

Answer:

QUESTION 3

A courier uses 8 litres of fuel to get to and from work each day. How much fuel is used if the same trip is completed 26 times?

Answer:

QUESTION 4

A jeweller has a sale on with the following items discounted: a ring that has half a carat of diamonds set in 18 ct gold for £849, a diamond-set pendant with a 9 ct gold chain for £145 and gold hoop earrings for £199. If a shopper buys two of each item, how much do they spend in total?

Answer:

QUESTION 5

At a greengrocer's, a shopper buys 4 green peppers for 99p each, 2 red onions for 45p each and 2 lettuces for £1.39 each. What is the total cost?

Answer:

QUESTION 6

A shopper purchases 16 bread rolls. If one bread roll costs 45p, how much do the 16 cost in total?

Answer:

QUESTION 7

A storeman's car uses 12 litres of diesel for every 100 miles driven. How much diesel would be used for 400 miles?

Answer:

QUESTION 8

A retail assistant earns £285 per month. If she earns the same amount each month, how much would she earn over a year?

Answer:

QUESTION 9

If 11 fridges are purchased each day in a large retail chain store, how many would be purchased over a 30-day month?

Answer:

QUESTION 10

If a car travels at 110 mph for 5 hours, how far has it travelled in total?

Answer:

Section D: Division

Short-answer questions

Specific instructions to students

- This section will help you to improve your division skills for basic operations.
- Read the following questions and answer all of them in the spaces provided.
- You need to show all working, you can use the blank Notes pages at the back of this book.

QUESTION 1

In a crowded store, 120 units of one item need to be stocked on 4 shelves. How many items will fit on each shelf?

Answer:

QUESTION 2

A store manager earns £785 for working a 5-day week. How much does she earn per day?

Answer:

QUESTION 3

A shop assistant in an electronics store needs to put out 24 packets of earphones onto 3 shelves. How many earphones will fit on each shelf?

Answer:

QUESTION 4

A whitegoods delivery van covers 780 miles in a 5-day week. How many miles per day has been travelled on average?

Answer:

QUESTION 5

A shipment of 30 computer workstations weighs 750 kilograms. How much does each computer workstation weigh?

Answer:

QUESTION 6

A sales representative travels 1825 miles over a 7-day period visiting retail outlets. Approximately how many miles are covered, on average, each day?

Answer:

QUESTION 7

At a yearly stock take, a storeperson counts 720 of the same toys. There are 12 toys in each box.

a   How many boxes are there?

Answer:

b   Are any toys left over?

Answer:

QUESTION 8

The manager of a children's store orders 480 wrestling figures. When they arrive, the manager discovers that there are 6 wrestling figures in each box. How many boxes are there?

Answer:

QUESTION 9

A furniture van carries 644 chairs to deliver to stores. The chairs are packed together in lots of 4. How many lots of chairs are there?

Answer:

QUESTION 10

Some hardware needs to be transported from a warehouse to a computer shop. The manager of the computer shop finds that 240 modems were delivered. If there are 3 modems in each lot, how many lots will there be?

Answer:

Section A: Introducing square numbers (L1)

Short-answer questions

Specific instructions to students

- This section is designed to help you to improve your skills and increase your speed in squaring numbers.
- Read the following questions and answer all of them in the spaces provided.
- You need to show all working, you can use the blank Notes pages at the back of this book.

> **Any number squared is multiplied by itself.**

EXAMPLE

4 squared $= 4^2 = 4 \times 4 = 16$

QUESTION 1

$6^2 =$

Answer:

QUESTION 2

$8^2 =$

Answer:

QUESTION 3

$12^2 =$

Answer:

QUESTION 4

$3^2 =$

Answer:

QUESTION 5

$7^2 =$

Answer:

QUESTION 6

$11^2 =$

Answer:

QUESTION 7

$10^2 =$

Answer:

QUESTION 8

$9^2 =$

Answer:

QUESTION 9

$2^2 =$

Answer:

QUESTION 10

$4^2 =$

Answer:

QUESTION 11

$5^2 =$

Answer:

Section B: Applying square numbers to Retail

Worded practical problems

Specific instructions to students

- This section is designed to help you to improve your skills and increase your speed in calculating volumes of rectangular or square objects. The worded questions make the content relevant to everyday situations.
- Read the following questions and answer all of them in the spaces provided.
- You need to show all working, you can use the blank Notes pages at the back of this book.

QUESTION 1

The table area for a book display measures 2.8 m × 2.8 m. What area does it take up?

Answer:

QUESTION 2

The area for a display board measures 2.2 m × 2.2 m. What is the total area?

Answer:

QUESTION 3

The dimensions of a function room at a hotel are 12.6 m × 12.6 m. What is the total area?

Answer:

QUESTION 4

A shop manager has an area for setting up an audio visual display that is 3.5 m × 3.5 m. How much area is this?

Answer:

QUESTION 5

A store has floor area available for presentations of goods which measures 23 m × 23 m. If the checkout area measures 3 m × 3 m, how much area is left?

Answer:

QUESTION 6

An assistant store manager has a sheet of advertising board that is 2.4 m × 1.2 m. If 30 cm × 30 cm is cut out for pop-out displays, how much is left for other advertising?

Answer:

QUESTION 7

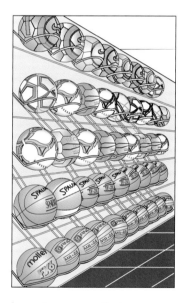

A sports store has a base area that measures 1.5 m × 1.5 m for a ball display. How much floor area does this take up?

Answer:

QUESTION 8

The base of a television advertising display measures 3.56 m × 3.56 m. What is the total area?

Answer:

_____

QUESTION 9

A mobile phone outlet has a floor area of 4.2 m × 4.2 m. What is the total area?

Answer:

_____

QUESTION 10

The walls of a major department store are to be decorated with advertising. The dimensions of the wall are 37 m × 37 m.

a What is the total wall area?

Answer:

_____

b If it costs £7.00 to paint one square metre, how much will it cost to paint 375 square metres?

Answer:

_____

Section A: Addition

Short-answer questions

Specific instructions to students

- This section will help you to improve your addition skills when working with decimals.
- Read the following questions and answer all of them in the spaces provided.
- You need to show all working, you can use the blank Notes pages at the back of this book.

QUESTION 1

A shopper buys a new mobile with a 24-month plan for £89.99, a new shirt for £36.50 and a DVD for £19.95. How much will the shopper pay in total?

Answer:

QUESTION 2

A family buys the following from a pet store: a puppy for £289.95, a kennel for £139.95 and pet food for £24.55. How much do the purchases come to in total?

Answer:

QUESTION 3

A cup holds 200 ml. If 30 ml of milk is added, as well as 20 ml of froth, what is the total?

Answer:

QUESTION 4

A curtain rail for a window measures 160.50 cm long and another is 80.5 cm. What is the total length of both?

Answer:

QUESTION 5

A shopper buys the following food: 5 kg of spaghetti for £8.99, a bottle of pasta sauce for £3.50 and 2 kg of mince for £12.50. What is the total cost?

Answer:

QUESTION 6

If a food delivery truck driver travels 65.8 miles, 36.5 miles, 22.7 miles and 89.9 miles, how far has been travelled in total?

Answer:

QUESTION 7

What is the total length of a shelf that measures 127.8 cm long that also has two attachment ends on it that each measure 10.5 cm?

Answer:

QUESTION 8

A bookcase has shelves that measure 35 cm, 32 cm, 38 cm and 42 cm in height. How tall is the bookcase?

Answer:

_____

QUESTION 9

Three pre-orders are being collected. The first order is worth £45.80, the second comes to £130.65 and the third is £116.45. How much is the total for all three?

Answer:

_____

QUESTION 10

A shopper orders some lunch which includes soup for £4.50, a main meal of chicken with salad for £8.50 and dessert that costs £5.50. What does the total bill come to?

Answer:

_____

Section B: Subtraction

Short-answer questions

Specific instructions to students

- This section will help you to improve your subtraction skills when working with decimals.
- Read the following questions and answer all of them in the spaces provided.
- You need to show all working, you can use the blank Notes pages at the back of this book.

QUESTION 1

A barista pours 250 ml from a 2-litre bottle of milk to make some hot drinks. How much milk is left in the bottle?

Answer:

_____

QUESTION 2

A sandwich-maker cuts off 2.5 cm of fat from a piece of bacon that is 31.4 cm long. How much bacon is left?

Answer:

_____

QUESTION 3

A customer orders a meal that costs £8.20. She then receives a discount of £1.50.

a   How much does the final bill come to?

Answer:

_____

b   How much change will she receive from £10.00?

_____

QUESTION 4

A shop assistant works 38 hours and earns £245.60. £29 is spent on petrol and £15 on a mobile phone top-up card. How much is left?

Answer:

_____

QUESTION 5

A group of 4 people each put in £10 for food and drinks. If the bill comes to £28.90, how much change will they receive?

Answer:

_____

QUESTION 6

A group of 3 friends go to the cinema. The cost of the tickets totals £41.50 and the total cost of popcorn and drinks comes to £26.50. If they have a total of £100.00, how much change will they have left?

Answer:

_____

QUESTION 7

At a computer store, a shopper purchases 3 computer games that cost a total of £32.50. How much change will he receive from £50.00?

Answer:

QUESTON 8

A driver buys 4 litres of engine oil. However, his car is slowly leaking oil, and after 3 months the car uses up 285 ml, 160 ml and 1300 ml of oil for each month respectively.

a   How much oil is used?

Answer:

b   How much is left?

Answer:

QUESTION 9

A bill for lunch includes £23.50 for 2 meals, £7.50 for a desert and £14.45 for 3 coffees.

a   What is the total cost?

Answer:

b   If the bill is paid with a £50 note, how much change is given?

Answer:

QUESTION 10

A set of knives are purchased for a café at a cost of £80.50. If it is paid for with two £50 notes, how much change will be given?

Answer:

Section C: Multiplication

Short-answer questions

Specific instructions to students

- This section will help you to improve your multiplication skills when working with decimals.
- Read the following questions and answer all of them in the spaces provided.
- You need to show all working, you can use the blank Notes pages at the back of this book.

QUESTION 1

A shopper goes to a sale where CDs are sold for £9.95. The shopper buys 6 CDs.

a   What is the total cost?

Answer:

b   How much change will the shopper receive from £70.00?

Answer:

QUESTION 2

A person buys 16 bottles of virgin olive oil. Each bottle costs £5.50.

a   What is the total cost for the 16 bottles?

Answer:

b   How much change will be received from two £50 notes?

Answer:

QUESTION 3

A consumer purchases 6 spice containers that cost £6.50 each and 4 bottles of pasta sauce at £3.95 per bottle.

a What is the total cost?

Answer:

_____

b How much change will the consumer receive from £55.00?

Answer:

_____

QUESTION 4

A group of 6 people dine at a restaurant that charges £16.50 per person for a banquet meal.

a How much is the total food bill?

Answer:

_____

b The diners tip the waiter £15.00. What does the total bill come to?

Answer:

_____

c How much change will they receive from £120.00?

Answer:

_____

QUESTION 5

Several supermarket workers go out for happy hour at the local pub. They have 9 cocktail drinks in total at a cost of £4.50 each.

a What is the total cost?

Answer:

_____

b How much change will they get from £50.00?

Answer:

_____

QUESTION 6

A starter consists of 3 steamed dim sims. Each dim sim costs £2.20.

a How much does the starter cost in total?

Answer:

_____

b How much change will the diners get from £10.00?

Answer:

_____

QUESTION 7

A canteen buys 120 pastries for £1.85 each. How much was spent in total?

Answer:

_____

QUESTION 8

A buyer places an order for 50 dozen oysters at £5.50 per dozen for a hotel.

a How much does the buyer pay in total?

Answer:

_____

b How much change will be needed from £300.00?

Answer:

_____

QUESTION 9

An event organizer orders 34 dinner rolls for a party.

a If each one costs £0.15, what is the outlay?

Answer:

_____

b How much change will she receive from £8.00?

Answer:

QUESTION 10

A hairdresser earns £130.65 per day before tax. How much is earned for a 5-day week?

Answer:

_____

Section D: Division

Short-answer questions

Specific instructions to students

- This section will help you to improve your division skills when working with decimals.
- Read the following questions and answer all of them in the spaces provided.
- You need to show all working, you can use the blank Notes pages at the back of this book.

QUESTION 1

A supermarket shopper purchases 12 eggs for a total of £3.60. How much does each individual egg cost?

Answer:

QUESTION 2

A store manager earns £990.50 for 5 days of work. How much does this work out to per day?

Answer:

QUESTION 3

A restaurant bill totals £455.70 for 8 people. How much does each person pay if they split the bill evenly?

Answer:

QUESTION 4

A food order at a bistro comes to £440.85 for 12 people. How much does each person pay if the bill is divided equally?

Answer:

QUESTION 5

A shoe shop serves 642 customers over 3 days during their summer sale. How many customers are served, on average, per day?

Answer:

QUESTION 6

A store assistant who works at chemist and delivers prescriptions travels 889.9 miles over 12 days. How far has been travelled, on average, each day?

Answer:

QUESTION 7

A sandwich van uses 11 litres of diesel to travel 257.3 miles. How far does the van travel per litre?

Answer:

QUESTION 8

A bag of flour weighing 2.5 kg is bought to be used in a recipe for 14 apple pies. How many grams of flour are needed per pie?

Answer:

QUESTION 10

A group of 5 people go to a deli. Each person in the group orders a chicken wrap, and the total comes to £31.60. How much does each person pay?

Answer:

QUESTION 9

A group of 3 students walk into a restaurant and order some coffee and muffins. The bill comes to £33.99. How much is the cost per person, if the bill is divided equally?

Answer:

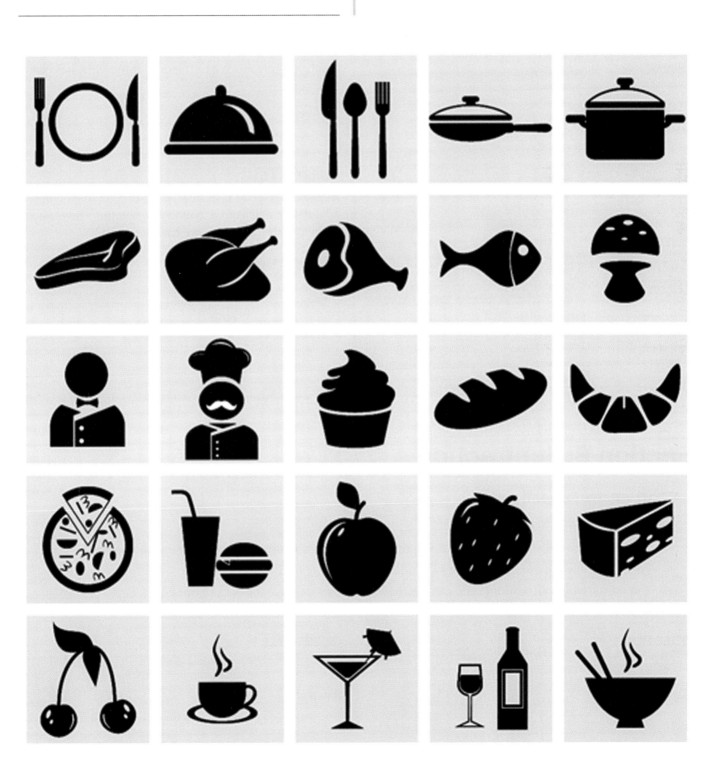

Section A: Addition

Short-answer questions

Specific instructions to students

- This section is designed to help you to improve your addition skills when working with fractions.
- Read the following questions and answer all of them in the spaces provided.
- You need to show all working, you can use the blank Notes pages at the back of this book.

QUESTION 1

$\frac{1}{2} + \frac{4}{5} =$

Answer:

_____

QUESTION 2

$1\frac{2}{3} + 1\frac{1}{2} =$

Answer:

_____

QUESTION 3

A carpet warehouse has 2 rolls of carpet. $\frac{1}{4}$ of a roll of Berber is left on one roll and $\frac{1}{3}$ of a roll of Berber is left on the other. How much Berber is there in total? Express your answer as a fraction.

Answer:

_____

QUESTION 4

An electronics store dedicates $\frac{1}{3}$ of the store to audio-visual and $\frac{2}{5}$ of the same store to mobile phone displays. How much as a fraction, of the store, has been taken up?

Answer:

_____

QUESTION 5

An ice cream shop uses $\frac{1}{3}$ of the counter for displaying advertising and $\frac{2}{4}$ of the counter for serving. How much of the counter, as a fraction, has been used?

Answer:

_____

Section B: Subtraction

Short-answer questions

Specific instructions to students

- This section is designed to help you to improve your subtraction skills when working with fractions.
- Read the following questions and answer all of them in the spaces provided.
- You need to show all working, you can use the blank Notes pages at the back of this book.

QUESTION 1

$\frac{2}{3} - \frac{1}{4} =$

Answer:

_____

QUESTION 2

$2\frac{2}{3} - 1\frac{1}{4} =$

Answer:

_____

QUESTION 3

A shop assistant has a shelf that is $\frac{2}{3}$ full of toys. If she removes $\frac{1}{3}$ of the toys from the shelf, how much room is left? Express your answer as a fraction.

Answer:

QUESTION 4

A newsagency has a shelf that is $\frac{2}{4}$ full of lifestyle magazines. If $\frac{1}{3}$ of the magazines are removed from the shelf, as they are out of date, how much of the shelf still has magazines? Express your answer as a fraction.

Answer:

QUESTION 5

A shop assistant working in a café has $2\frac{1}{4}$ cartons of milk on Monday to serve customers. A further $1\frac{1}{3}$ cartons of milk are used over Tuesday and Wednesday. How much milk is left? Express your answer as a fraction.

Answer:

Section C: Ratio, Scale and Proportion

Short-answer questions

Specific instructions to students

- In this unit, you will improve your skills in working out ratios, scale and proportion.
- Read the following questions and answer all of them in the spaces provided.
- You need to show all working, you can use the blank Notes pages at the back of this book.

QUESTION 1

The label on a large bottle of juice in the supermarket where you work states 'Dilute 1 part juice to 3 parts water'. How much water must be added to 2 litres of juice?

(1) 1.3 litres

(2) 6 litres

(3) 8 litres

(4) 0.3 litres

Answer:

QUESTION 2

A recipe for 4 fruit scones requires the following ingredients:

| 200 g flour |
| 2 eggs |
| 100 ml milk |
| 50 g currants |

How much flour is needed to make 6 fruit scones?

(1) 1200 g

(2) 600 g

(3) 30 g

(4) 300 g

Answer:

QUESTION 3

A market stall worker is making muffins to sell at a village fair. His recipe for 36 muffins requires the following ingredients:

| 900 g flour |
| 3 level tsp baking powder |
| 270 g sugar |
| 750 ml milk |
| 6 eggs |
| 12 tbsp sunflower oil |

How much flour does he need to make 72 muffins?

(1) 30 g

(2) 1400 g

(3) 1800 g

(4) 500 g

Answer:

QUESTION 4

Due to falling profit, 600 shop workers lose their jobs. 480 of these are women. What is the ratio of men to women who lose their jobs?

(1) 4:1

(2) 5:1

(3) 1:4

(4) 10:6

Answer:

QUESTION 5

For every 1000 toys manufactured 50 are rejected. What is the ratio of failed toys to successful toys?

(1) 19:1

(2) 1:19

(3) 3:30

(4) 4:20

Answer:

QUESTION 6

A lorry driver lives 1 km away from his depot. It takes him 30 minutes to walk to there. What is his walking speed?

(1) 2 km per hour

(2) 4 m per hour

(c) 4 m per half an hour

(4) 2 km per half hour

Answer:

QUESTION 7

Catherine and Suzannah spend £5 between them on their lottery tickets each week at work. Catherine puts in £1 and Suzannah puts in £4. They have agreed to share the winnings according to the amount they put in. One week they win £45 000. How much will they get each?

(1) Catherine will get £15 000 and Suzannah will get £30 000

(2) Catherine will get £11 000 and Suzannah will get £34 000

(3) Catherine will get £10 000 and Suzannah will get £35 000

(4) Catherine will get £9000 and Suzannah will get £36 000

Answer:

QUESTION 8

Jack needs to make enough fruit punch for the staff party. It is estimated that 80 people will be attending. For 20 glasses the recipe needs 50 ml of lemon juice. How much lemon juice does he need for 80 glasses?

(1) 150 ml

(2) 50 ml

(3) 200 ml

(4) 500 ml

Answer:

QUESTION 9

Following the recommendations of the British Heart Foundation, your retail tutor wants to incorporate 2 hours of exercise into each week's study time. You do 5 hours study per week with the retail tutor, so what will be the ratio of exercise time against study time?

(1) 2:3

(2) 3:2

(3) 4:2

(4) 6:2

Answer:

QUESTION 10

The college decides to take 20 students on a retail trip. For safety reasons, the ratio of adults to students must be at least 1:10. How many adults are required for the trip?

(1) 7

(2) 6

(3) 2

(4) 5

Answer:

_____

QUESTION 11

The entire group (adults and students) go to the shopping centre in cars. Each car is driven by an extra volunteer and can hold 4 passengers. How many cars would they need altogether?

(1) 10

(2) 7

(3) 9

(4) 5

Answer:

_____

QUESTION 12

You invite your colleagues home for a spicy curry. If the recipe you normally use for 4 people uses $\frac{3}{4}$ of a teaspoon of curry powder, how many teaspoons of curry powder do you need for 10 times the quantity?

(1) 8 teaspoons

(2) 6.5 teaspoons

(3) 10 teaspoons

(4) 7.5 teaspoons

Answer:

_____

QUESTION 13

The supermarket you work in has asked you to make a lemon tart for a cookery demonstration. The recipe is:

Buttery Lemon Tart (serves 8)

150 g plain flour

20 tbsp lemon juice

10 tbsp water

grated rind of 3 lemons

125 g butter

125 g caster sugar

4 eggs

a   What is the ratio of lemon juice to water in its simplest form? Show your working.

Answer:

_____

b   How many ingredients would you need for 12 people?

Answer:

_____

_____

_____

c   How much butter is needed for a larger flan that uses 25 tbsp water? Show your working.

Answer:

_____

QUESTION 14

Carole makes green paint for painting the training room by mixing yellow and blue in the ratio 1:4.

a   How much yellow paint does she use with 4 tins of blue? Show your working.

Answer:

_____

b   How much blue paint does she use with 16 tins of yellow? Show your working.

Answer:

_____

QUESTION 15

Carole makes a fruit cocktail drink for the staff party using orange juice and apple juice in the ratio 3:2.

a   How much apple juice does she mix with 9 litres orange juice? Show your working.

Answer:

_____

b   How much orange juice does she mix with 12 litres apple juice? Show your working.

Answer:

_____

QUESTION 16

Tracey invites three colleagues around for a meal after work. She makes smoked ham linguine. For 4 people the recipe requires 450 g dried linguine.

a   How much linguine would she need if she invited all 11 of her colleagues? Show your working.

Answer:

_____

b   How much linguine would she need if she invited all their partners as well? Show your working.

Answer:

_____

QUESTION 17

Susan decides to make enough spinach soup to take to work for the whole week. For 4 people the recipe needs 400g of spinach, which would last her 4 days. However, she is working 7 days. How much spinach does she need to make the soup last the whole week? Show your working.

Answer:

_____

QUESTION 18

Michael is paid £10.50 per hour working as a Health and Safety Officer.

a   How much is he paid for 20 hours' work? Show your working.

Answer:

_____

b   How much is he paid for 40 hours' work? Show your working.

Answer:

_____

QUESTION 19

Peter works as a sales manager and goes out to see customers 3 days out of 5. He earns £300 for the 3 days he is out of the office and £160 for the days he is in the office. His hours of work are 9 a.m. to 5 p.m. with 1 hour unpaid for lunch.

a   How much does he get paid per hour when he is in the office? Show your working.

Answer:

_____

_____

_____

b   How much does he get paid per hour when he is on the road? Show your working.

Answer:

_____

_____

_____

QUESTION 20

You are taking a holiday from work to go to Amsterdam and Rotterdam. The actual distance between the two cities is 58 km. What is the distance between these two cities on a map when the scale on the map is 1cm = 10 km? Show your working.

Answer:

_____

_____

Unit 12: Percentages

Short-answer questions

Specific instructions to students

- In this unit, you will be able to practise and improve your skills in working out percentages.
- Read the following questions and answer all of them in the spaces provided.
- You need to show all working, you can use the blank Notes pages at the back of this book.

> **10% rule: Move the decimal one place to the left to get 10%.**

EXAMPLE

10% of £45.00 would be £4.50

QUESTION 1

A shopper buys a pair of jeans at a department store and the bill comes to £220.00, without the 10% off sale discount.

a   How much is the 10% discount worth?

Answer:

_____

b   What does the final price of the jeans come to?

Answer:

_____

QUESTION 2

A sales assistant in a computer store sells a laptop for £350.00 without a 10% off discount.

a   How much will the discount be?

Answer:

_____

b   What does the sale total after the 10% discount is taken off the bill?

Answer:

_____

QUESTION 3

An air-conditioning company offers a 10% discount on a 2 hp air conditioner the air conditioner is priced at £698.50 before the discount.

a   How much is the discount worth to the customer?

Answer:

_____

QUESTION 4

A store manager sells 2-litre bottles of cordial at £2.80 each. A 5% price discount is given to help sell the bottles quickly due to a short best-before date.

a   How much is the 5% price reduction worth?

Answer:

_____

b   How much does the cordial bottle cost after the 5% price reduction? (Hint: find 10%, halve it to find 5%, then subtract it from £2.80.)

Answer:

_____

QUESTION 5

A student buys 3 roller storage bins for £20, a jacket for £69 and a DVD box set of £89. When the student goes to pay at the till, she discovers that there is a 10% discount that applies to all of her purchased items.

a   How much does the bill come to in total before the discount?

Answer:

_____

b   How much does the bill total after the 10% discount?

Answer:

_____

QUESTION 6

The following items are purchased as Christmas presents: a pair of shorts for £39.99, a lamp for £19.99, a new shirt for £19.50, a mobile phone for £99.00, a set of weights for £189.00 and some gardening tools for £14.25.

a   What is the total cost of the goods purchased?

Answer:

b   What is the final cost after a 10% discount is given?

Answer:

c   How much change would be received from £400.00?

Answer:

QUESTION 7

A food store offers 20% off the price of all its chocolate products. The cost of 4 items comes to £59.80 before the discount.

a   How much is the 20% discount worth?

Answer:

b   What is the price of the four chocolate products after the 20% discount?

Answer:

c   What change would be given from £70.00?

Answer:

QUESTION 8

The regular retail price of a pair of shoes is £85.60. There is a 15% discounted sale on at the moment in the shoe store.

a   How much is the 15% discount worth?

Answer:

b   What does the final sales price come to?

Answer:

c   How much change would you get back from £100.00?

Answer:

QUESTION 9

A nut store has a 20% discount sale. A shopper passing by sees a packet of cashew nuts priced at £3.20.

a   How much is the 20% discount worth?

Answer:

b   How much will the nuts cost after the 20% discount?

Answer:

c   What change would be needed from £10.00?

Answer:

QUESTION 10

A group of 5 people purchase cinema tickets at a cost of £70.00. The group also buys popcorn and drinks costing £42.60. One person has a voucher for 20% off the total price of the cinema tickets.

a   How much is the 20% discount off the cinema tickets worth?

Answer:

b   How much change would the group get back from £100.00?

Answer:

Short-answer questions

Specific instructions to students

- This unit is designed to help you to both improve your skills and to increase your speed in converting one measurement unit into another.
- Read the following questions and answer all of them in the spaces provided.
- You need to show all working, you can use the blank Notes pages at the back of this book.

QUESTION 1

How many centimetres are there in 1 metre?

Answer:

_____

QUESTION 2

How many millimetres are there in 1 metre?

Answer:

_____

QUESTION 3

How many centimetres are there in 11 metres?

Answer:

_____

QUESTION 4

How many pence are there in £3.75?

Answer:

_____

QUESTION 5

How many pence are there in £10.83?

Answer:

_____

QUESTION 6

How many centimetres are there in 1.25 metres of material?

Answer:

_____

QUESTION 7

How many grams are in 1.2 kilograms of washing powder?

Answer:

_____

QUESTION 8

How many millilitres are in 1.5 litres of soft drink?

Answer:

_____

QUESTION 9

How many centimetres are in 1560 mm of pine?

Answer:

_____

QUESTION 10

How many centimetres in 5850 millimetres of timber?

Answer:

_____

Section A: Circumference

Short-answer questions

Specific instructions to students

- This section is designed to help you to both improve your skills and to increase your speed in measuring the circumference of a round object.
- Read the following questions and answer all of them in the spaces provided.
- You need to show all working, you can use the blank Notes pages at the back of this book.

$C = \pi \times d$

where:

C = circumference

π = 3.14

d = diameter

EXAMPLE

Find the circumference of a plate with a diameter of 30 cm.

$C = \pi \times d$

Therefore, $C = 3.14 \times 30$

$= 94.2$ cm

QUESTION 1

Find the circumference of a display table with a diameter of 90 cm.

Answer:

QUESTION 2

Calculate the circumference of a display board with a diameter of 15 cm.

Answer:

QUESTION 3

Find the circumference of a diamond ring with a diameter of 3 cm.

Answer:

QUESTION 4

Find the circumference of a chopping board with a diameter of 100 cm.

Answer:

QUESTION 5

Find the circumference of flood light with a diameter of 12 cm.

Answer:

QUESTION 6

Calculate the circumference of a CD with a diameter of 22 cm.

Answer:

QUESTION 7

Find the circumference of a Tupperware container with a diameter of 15.6 cm.

Answer:

QUESTION 8

Find the circumference of a kitchen extractor fan with a diameter of 14.3 cm.

Answer:

QUESTION 9

Find the circumference of a smoke alarm with a diameter of 12.9 cm.

Answer:

QUESTION 10

Calculate the circumference of a starter plate with a diameter of 18.8 cm.

Answer:

Section B: Diameter

Short-answer questions

Specific instructions to students

- This section is designed to help you to both improve your skills and to increase your speed in measuring the diameter of a round object.
- Read the following questions and answer all of them in the spaces provided.
- You need to show all working, you can use the blank Notes pages at the back of this book.

Diameter (d) of a circle $= \dfrac{\text{circumference}}{\pi\,(3.14)}$

EXAMPLE

Find the diameter of a display table with a circumference of 800 cm.

$d = \dfrac{800}{3.14}$

$\quad = 254.78$ cm

QUESTION 1

Find the diameter of a round mirror with a circumference of 120 cm.

Answer:

QUESTION 2

Determine the diameter of a wheel cover with a circumference of 600 cm.

Answer:

QUESTION 3

Calculate the diameter of a hotplate with a circumference of 50 cm.

Answer:

QUESTION 4

Find the diameter of a basin with a circumference of 200 cm.

Answer:

QUESTION 5

Calculate the diameter of a cut-off saw with a circumference of 430 cm.

Answer:

QUESTION 6

Find the diameter of a skylight with a circumference 140 cm.

Answer:

QUESTION 7

Determine the diameter of a glass feature window with a circumference of 135 cm.

Answer:

QUESTION 8

Calculate the diameter of a round table with a circumference of 280 cm.

Answer:

QUESTION 9

Find the diameter of a microwave dish with a circumference of 62 cm.

Answer:

QUESTION 10

Calculate the diameter of a deep fat fryer with a circumference of 68 cm.

Answer:

Section C: Area and perimeter

Short-answer questions

Specific instructions to students

- This section is designed to help you to both improve your skills and to increase your speed in measuring surface area and perimeters.
- Read the following questions and answer all of them in the spaces provided.
- You need to show all working, you can use the blank Notes pages at the back of this book.

> **Area = length × breadth and is given in square units.**
> **= $l \times b$**

QUESTION 1

The dimensions of a cooking tray sold in a homeware shop are 30 cm long by 12.8 cm wide. What is the total area of the tray?

Answer:

QUESTION 2

If the shop floor measures 20 m by 13 m, what is the total area?

Answer:

QUESTION 3

The dimensions of a display area is 2.85 m by 1.65 m. What is the total area?

Answer:

QUESTION 4

An area set aside to display toys measures 14.5 m by 12.8 m. What is the total area?

Answer:

_____

QUESTION 5

What is the total area of a market stall that displays men's, women's and children's clothing that measures 13 m by 9 m?

Answer:

_____

QUESTION 6

A hardware warehouse measures 335 m by 230 m. What is the total area?

Answer:

_____

QUESTION 7

If a jewellery store's floor area is 12.06 m by 8.07 m, what is the total area?

Answer:

_____

QUESTION 8

If a newsagent has a floor space of 6.53 m by 3.27 m, how much floor area is there?

Answer:

_____

QUESTION 9

A whitegoods store allocates a display area for sinks, washing machines and bathroom accessories that is 38.2 m by 21.6 m. What is the total area?

Answer:

_____

QUESTION 10

A fruit juice shop is 8.9 m long and 2.6 m wide. How much floor area is there?

Answer:

_____

QUESTION 11

The perimeter is the distance around a shape.

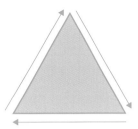

a   What are the perimeters of the following shapes?

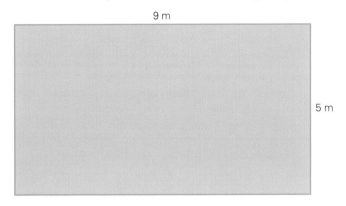

Answer:

_____

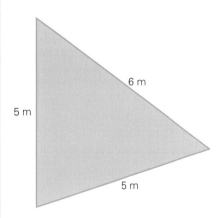

Answer:

_____

b   The building you work in measures 116 m × 77 m. Your sister works in a building measuring 114 m × 75 m. Work out the perimeter of each building.

Answer:

_____

_____

c   How do you find the area of a square or a rectangle?

Answer:

_____

d Find the missing lengths of the following shapes, then calculate the area of each shape.

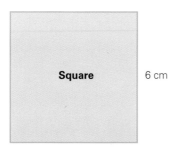

Square   6 cm

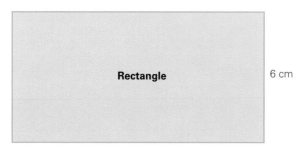

Rectangle   6 cm

12 cm

Answer:

_____

_____

e Find the area of the following shape. **Remember, when you have different units (e.g. cm and m) you must** convert them to the same units before you calculate area.

1.5 m

50 cm

Answer:

_____

f Complete the table below.

Shape	Number of sides	Number of corners
square	4	4
circle		
rectangle		
oval		0
triangle		

QUESTION 12

A colleague is retiring from the supermarket and your boss is going to hold a surprise buffet at the Old Hall Hotel. You are liaising with the pastry chef, who needs to be economical and not waste too much pastry. The pastry he makes will be rolled out into a rectangular sheet measuring 297 mm by 420 mm.

He will be making:

- canapés – made out of pastry circles measuring 30 mm in diameter

- tartlets – made out of pastry circles measuring 120 mm in diameter

- mini quiches – made out of pastry circles measuring 180 mm in diameter

- samosas – made out of pastry circles measuring 100 mm in diameter

- vol-au-vents – made out of pastry circles measuring 50 mm in diameter

How many of each item will the chef get out of one sheet of pastry? Complete the table below. You might need to draw a sketch to help you.

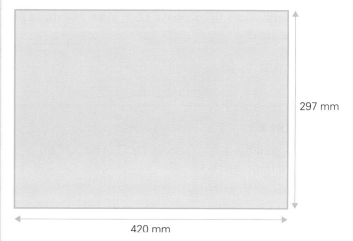

297 mm

420 mm

Thing about these questions will help you:

- How many of each pastry shape would fit along the long edge of the pastry?

- How many of each pastry shape would fit along the short edge of the pastry?

Pastry item	Diameter	Number out of one sheet of pastry
Canapé		
Tartlet		
Mini quiche		
Samosa		
Vol-au-vent		

Section D: Volume of a cube

Short-answer questions

Specific instructions to students

- This section is designed to help you to both improve your skills and to increase your speed in calculating volumes of rectangular or square objects.
- Read the following questions and answer all of them in the spaces provided.
- You need to show all working, you can use the blank Notes pages at the back of this book.

> **Volume = length × width × height and is given in cubic units.**
> **= l × w × h**

QUESTION 1

How many cubic metres are there in an electrical retail outlet storage area 30 m long by 35 m wide by 4 m high?

Answer:

QUESTION 2

A cold storage delivery truck has the dimensions of 8 m in length by 3 m of width by 4 m of height. How many cubic metres are available?

Answer:

QUESTION 3

A refrigerated cold room measures 8 m × 3 m × 2 m. How many cubic metres are there?

Answer:

QUESTION 4

If an Italian restaurant uses a cooking tray for lasagne that measures 22 cm by 18 cm by 5 cm, how many cubic centimetres can it hold?

Answer:

QUESTION 5

A retail assistant uses a display case with the following dimensions: 60 cm by 15 cm by 10 cm. How many cubic centimetres can it hold?

Answer:

QUESTION 6

The back of a truck measures 2.8 m × 1.5 m × 2.2. What cubic area is available to use for storing goods?

Answer:

QUESTION 7

A storage box used by a retail store is 1m long, 60 cm wide and 75 cm tall. How many cubic centimetres are available for storage?

Answer:

QUESTION 8

A jewellery display cabinet is 90 cm wide by 1 m long by 80 cm high. How much cubic area does it contain?

Answer:

QUESTION 9

A shelf in a major department store has the following dimensions: 0.75 m × 0.85 m × 2.6 m. What is its volume in cubic metres?

Answer:

QUESTION 10

An audio visual display cabinet is 2.8 m long by 1 m wide by 1.1 m high. How many cubic metres are available for displaying items?

Answer:

Section E: Volume of a cylinder

Short-answer questions

Specific instructions to students

- This section is designed to help you to both improve your skills and to increase your speed in calculating volumes of cylinder-shaped objects.
- Read the following questions and answer all of them in the spaces provided.
- You need to show all working, you can use the blank Notes pages at the back of this book.

Volume of a cylinder $(V_c) = \pi\ (3.14) \times r^2$
(radius $\times$ radius) $\times$ height

$V_c = \pi \times r^2 \times h$

QUESTION 1

What is the volume of a can that has a radius of 5 cm and a height of 14 cm?

Answer:

QUESTION 2

What is the volume of an ice cream tub that has a radius of 15 cm and a height of 90 cm?

Answer:

QUESTION 3

A double action pump has a radius of 14 cm and a height of 45 cm. What volume of air can be pumped?

Answer:

QUESTION 4

A large coffee can used in a coffee shop has a radius of 12 cm and a height of 28 cm. How much coffee can it hold?

Answer:

QUESTION 5

A large soup can has a radius of 13 cm and a height of 26 cm. What is its volume?

Answer:

QUESTION 6

A gas bottle used for cooking a barbeque has a radius of 17 cm and a height of 60 cm. How much gas could it hold?

Answer:

QUESTION 7

A large container of vegetable oil used in a restaurant is poured into 3 containers. Each container has a radius of 8 cm and a height of 20 cm.

a What is the volume of each container?

Answer:

b What is the volume of all 3 containers in total?

Answer:

QUESTION 8

A container used for pool chlorine has a radius of 10 cm and a height of 55 cm.

a   What is its volume?

Answer:

b   If half is used up during summer, how much is left?

Answer:

QUESTION 9

A water bottle has a radius of 8 cm and a height of 22 cm.

a   What is its volume?

Answer:

_____

b   If you use half during the day, how much is left?

Answer:

_____

QUESTION 10

A container for children's toys has a radius of 26 cm and a height of 80 cm. What is its volume?

Answer:

_____

Section F: Algebra and formulae

Short-answer questions

Specific instructions to students

- This section is designed to help you to both improve your skills and to increase your speed in using algebra and formulae in calculations.
- Read the following questions and answer all of them in the spaces provided.
- You need to show all working, you can use the blank Notes pages at the back of this book.

Algebra is the use of letters and symbols to represent numbers. Formulas (called formulae) often use algebra. Examples of formulae are:

Circumference of a circle $= \pi d$

Volume of a cuboid $= l \times w \times h$ (or, lwh)

Perimeter of a rectangle $= 2(l + w)$

With formulae, if there is no 'instruction' between one symbol and the next, ALWAYS assume you MULTIPLY. For example:

$ABC = A \times B \times C$

$5(E + F) = 5 \times (E + F)$

With formulae you may be given the values of the letters. You then solve the problem by taking the letters out, and putting in the actual values of those letters. This is called substitution.

The area of a circle is given by the formula $A = \pi r^2$.

A = area of the circle, $\pi = 3.14$, r = radius of circle.

To work out the area of a circle with a radius of 5 cm, you are working out A (the area). You know $\pi = 3$ and $r = 5$. There is no instruction between π and r^2, so $\pi r^2 = \pi \times r^2$. You can now substitute the values for the letters.

$$A = \pi \times r^2$$
$$= 3 \times 5^2$$
$$= 3 \times 25$$
$$= 75 \text{ cm}^2$$

So the area of a circle with radius 5 cm is 75 cm².

Now answer the following questions using formulae and algebra.

QUESTION 1

a   Calculate the perimeter. Remember: Perimeter $= 2(l + w)$. l = length, w = width

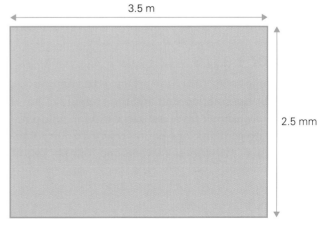

3.5 m

2.5 mm

Answer:

_____

b   Calculate the area. Remember: Area = l × w.

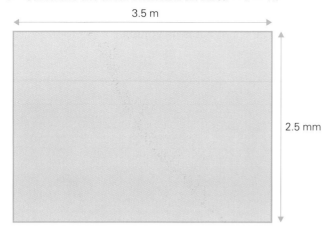

3.5 m

2.5 mm

Answer:

_____

c   In a supermarket, if gross profit = sales − food cost
Calculate the gross profit of the following:

sales = £25   food cost = £15   gross profit = _____

sales = £57   food cost = £31   gross profit = _____

d   My monthly mobile phone charges are calculated
using the following formula:
Cost = £15 + £0.20 × minutes used
How much will it cost for:

i)   30 minutes used = _____

ii)   70 minutes used = _____

iii)   140 minutes used = _____

QUESTION 2

You work for a company that wishes to promote a new
product and you need to produce some leaflets to give
out to the public. The printer has given you the cost of
printing based on the following formula.

C = 27 + 0.4 × N

(C = cost in £ and N = number of leaflets)

a   What is the cost of producing 50 leaflets?

Answer:

_____

b   What is the cost of producing 1000 leaflets?

Answer:

_____

c   If you only have £30, how many leaflets can you get
printed? Show your working.

Answer:

_____

_____

Section G: Probability

Short-answer questions

Specific instructions to students

- This section is designed to help you to both improve your skills and to increase your speed in calculating
probabilities.
- Read the following questions and answer all of them in the spaces provided.
- You need to show all working, you can use the blank Notes pages at the back of this book.

Summer Fayre

You and some colleagues have organized a summer
fayre for all supermarket staff and their families. One of
the stalls at a summer fayre is a lucky dip for children.
The lucky dip contains: one pound coin, two 50p coins,
three 10p coins, two tubes of sweets and four packets of
chocolate.

QUESTION 1

a   What is the probability that the first child will pick
some money?

Answer:

_____

_____

b   What is the probability that the first child will pick a
50p coin?

Answer:

_____

_____

c What is the probability that the first child will pick a tube of sweets?

Answer:

_____

_____

d What is the probability that the first child will pick a packet of chocolate?

Answer:

_____

_____

e What is the probability that the first child will pick something edible?

Answer:

_____

_____

f What is the probability that the first child will pick something other than a 10p coin?

Answer:

_____

_____

_____

QUESTION 2

The first child picks the pound coin.

a What is the probability that the second child will pick some money?

Answer:

_____

_____

_____

_____

b What is the probability that the second child will pick a 50p coin?

Answer:

_____

c What is the probability that the second child will pick a packet of sweets?

Answer:

_____

_____

QUESTION 3

The second child picks a 10p coin

a What is the probability that the third child will pick a packet of sweets?

Answer:

_____

_____

_____

_____

_____

_____

b What is the probability that the third child will pick some money?

Answer:

_____

_____

c What is the probability that the third child will pick a 10p coin?

Answer:

_____

_____

d What is the probability that the third child will pick a pound coin?

Answer:

_____

_____

Short-answer questions

Specific instructions to students

- This unit will help you to calculate how much a job is worth, and how long you need to complete the job.
- Read the following questions and answer all of them in the spaces provided.
- You need to show all working, you can use the blank Notes pages at the back of this book.

QUESTION 1

A shop assistant earns £98.50 clear per week for 10 hours work. How much does she earn per year, given that she works the same number of hours each week? (Note also that there are 52 weeks in a year.)

Answer:

QUESTION 2

A checkout assistant starts a shift at a department store at 10.00 a.m. and stops for a break at 1.30 p.m. He starts again at 2.00 p.m. then finishes the shift at 4.15 p.m.

a   How many hours and minutes has he worked?

Answer:

b   How much will he earn if he gets paid £8.20 per hour?

Answer:

QUESTION 3

A waitress earns £5.50 an hour and works a 38-hour week. How much are her gross earnings (before tax)?

Answer:

QUESTION 4

Over a 6-day week, the takings for a coffee shop are: £465.80, £2490.50, £556.20, £1560.70 and £990.60. What are the total takings?

Answer:

QUESTION 5

A chef needs the following amount of time to cook 5 orders: 14 minutes, 11 minutes, 7 minutes, 15 minutes and 9 minutes. How much time has been spent on cooking the orders? State your answer in hours and minutes.

Answer:

QUESTION 6

A department store café worker prepares food for lunch. The tasks take $4\frac{1}{2}$ hours to complete. If the café worker gets £9.60 an hour, how much will she earn during this time?

Answer:

QUESTION 7

Over a shift a shop assistant spends $3\frac{1}{2}$ hours stocking shelves and $2\frac{1}{2}$ hours working on the front counter. If the shop assistant gets paid £11.80 per hour, how much does she earn during this shift?

Answer:

QUESTION 8

A buffet needs to be prepared in advance by the kitchen staff. They take 3.5 hours preparing the food for the buffet, 1.5 hours preparing and decorating the tables and 0.5 hours preparing drinks. How long in hours and minutes has all of the preparations taken?

Answer:

_____

QUESTION 9

A cook starts work at 7.00 a.m. to prepare breakfast and works until 3.00 p.m. He has a morning break that lasts for 20 minutes, a lunch break for 60 minutes and an afternoon break of 20 minutes.

a   How much time has he spent on breaks?

Answer:

_____

b   How much time has he spent working?

Answer:

_____

QUESTION 10

The total cost of a bulk purchase of books for a bookstore is £2850.50. If it took 12 hours to prepare, load and deliver the books, how much is the rate per hour?

Answer:

_____

QUESTION 11

Oxfam is a not-for-profit retailer and requires volunteers to work for nothing. However, if the volunteers worked in a department store, they would be paid £6.00 an hour. How much would they receive for an 8-hour day?

Answer:

_____

QUESTION 12

Fill in the gaps on the timesheet, using the instructions and information below.

Jane works a 5-hour shift.

Alison works for 4.5 hours.

What time does Abigail sign out?

Emma works for 11 hours and 45 minutes and gets paid £2.50 per hour less than Alison.

Tania earns £1.75 more per hour than Jane and works for 7.5 hours with a half hour unpaid break in the middle of her shift.

Name	Time in	Time out	Rate of pay	Total
Jane	10:00		£6.50	
Alison		12:30	£10.45	£47.03
Abigail	7:45		£7.50	£33.75
Emma		16:00		
Tania	13:50			

Short-answer questions

Specific instructions to students

- This unit will help you to solve problems requiring calculations.
- Read the following questions and answer all of them in the spaces provided.
- You need to show all working, you can use the blank Notes pages at the back of this book.

There are many different options customers can choose from to pay for a purchase. Many stores offer a discounted 'deal' for a product if you buy it on the spot, or you could pay for it over a certain time period, such as over four years. Alternatively, other stores offer the products for hire. But what is the difference in the final amount paid between the two payment options?

EXAMPLE

A wall of built-in wardrobes retails at £3191. The 4-year or 48-month plan means that the buyer pays £27.15 per week over 4 years.

£27.15 (per week)

    × 52 (52 weeks over 1 year)

    = £1411.80 (total over 1 year)

then

    × 4 (over 4 years)

    = £5647.20 (total paid)

Therefore:

4-year/48-month plan price: £5647.20

Retail price = £3191.00

Difference = £2456.20

Therefore, the difference is an extra £2456.20 that would need to be paid off over 4 years.

QUESTION 1

A matching bed and chest of drawers retail for £2997. The 4-year or 48-month payment plan means that the buyer pays £25.50 per week over 4 years. What is the price difference between the two payment options?

Answer:

_____

QUESTION 2

A sofa retails for £898. The 4-year or 48-month payment plan means that the buyer pays £7.64 per week over 4 years. What is the price difference between the two payment options?

Answer:

_____

QUESTION 3

A freestanding kitchen retails for £4997. The 4-year or 48-month payment plan means that the buyer pays £45.52 per week over 4 years. What is the price difference between the two payment options?

Answer:

_____

QUESTION 4

A set of dining tables and chairs retails for £1596. The 4-year or 48-month payment plan means that the buyer pays £13.58 per week over 4 years. What is the price difference between the two payment options?

Answer:

_____

QUESTION 5

A fitted kitchen retails for £5998. The 4-year or 48-month payment plan means that the buyer pays £51.04 per week over 4 years. What is the price difference between the two payment options?

Answer:

QUESTION 6

A set of designer outdoor furniture retails for £2997. The 4-year or 48-month payment plan means that the buyer pays £25.50 per week over 4 years. What is the price difference between the two payment options?

Answer:

QUESTION 7

An ultra-thin laptop computer retails for £898. The 4-year or 48-month payment plan means that the buyer pays £7.64 per week over 4 years. What is the price difference between the two payment options?

Answer:

QUESTION 8

A 15″ notebook laptop computer retails for £645. The store has a 'cashback' offer which means that the final cost will be £496. How much is the 'cashback' offer worth?

Answer:

QUESTION 9

A desktop computer retails for £1962. There is an option to rent/buy plan for £17.80 per week.

a   How many weeks would it take until the retail price is reached?

Answer:

b   If it was purchased over 36 months, how much more would you pay than if you bought it outright?

Answer:

QUESTION 10

A desktop computer retails for £1525. There is an option to rent/buy plan for £15.50 per week. If it was purchased over 36 months, how much more would you pay than if you bought it outright?

Answer:

Short-answer questions

Specific instructions to students

- This unit will help you to calculate the details of invoices and bills.
- Read the following questions and answer all of them in the spaces provided.
- You need to show all working, you can use the blank Notes pages at the back of this book.

QUESTION 1

A customer makes an appointment to see a personal shopper in a department store. The total comes to £350. The store has had a promotion in the local paper that reduces the cost by 20% for one month only.

a By how much does the personal shopper need to adjust the final bill?

Answer:

b How much will the final cost be?

Answer:

QUESTION 2

A customer books their holiday insurance through the Post Office. The customer receives a 10% discount due to a promotion that the Post Office is having.

a If the insurance costs £55.00, how much will the Post Office need to take off due to the 10% discount?

Answer:

b How much will the insurance cost after the discount?

Answer:

QUESTION 3

A wholesaler charges £20.50 for delivery to a small retail outlet. The wholesaler was called out three times this week, so how much will the invoice be for the small retailer for delivery costs?

Answer:

QUESTION 4

A customer is charged for having their food delivered by van, which is £7.50 on a Sunday. When the van driver arrives at the house 2 hours late, the customer demands the delivery fee be removed from the invoice. The bill came to £150.01. How much is the invoice now?

Answer:

QUESTION 5

An online retailer called playtoday.com sells CDs at £5.00 each on a Wednesday and Sunday. Michael purchases 2 on Wednesday and 5 on Sunday. The postage is £2.40 per order. How much is the final bill?

Answer:

QUESTION 6

A mobile phone shop receives the following goods: masking tape for £12.60, a new printer for £145.00 and 50 vertical files with tabs for £39.95. A 15% voucher is included as a one-off special for an end-of-financial-year sale.

a How much is the total before the discount?

Answer:

b How much is the discount?

Answer:

c What is the final cost?

Answer:

QUESTION 7

A department store purchases office supplies. The goods total £224. A '25% off' sale is on.

a How much is saved?

Answer:

b What is the final cost?

Answer:

QUESTION 8

Office furniture is purchased by an assistant manager for a confectionery store. The total cost is £1121.50. A '10% off' voucher is used.

a How much is the voucher worth?

Answer:

b What is the final cost?

Answer:

QUESTION 9

Three different wholesalers make purchases at an office supplies store. Each one also has a '15% off' voucher. The first wholesaler purchases a hole punch, filing cabinets, pens, folders and envelopes, spending a total of £264. The second wholesaler purchases office furniture, masking tape, highlighter pens, whiteboard markers and vertical files for a total of £158. The third wholesaler purchases graph books, lined books, a petty cash box, and manila and display folders, all for £88.

a How much is the total purchases for all three wholesalers without the voucher?

Answer:

b How much will the voucher decrease the cost for each wholesaler?

Answer:

c What is the final cost for each of the three wholesalers?

Answer:

d What is the total of the three wholesalers' purchases after the discount?

Answer:

QUESTION 10

A department store decides to reward its last five 'Employees of the Month'. The retail manager books rooms at a hotel for 7 nights in Spain. The cost per person per night is £95.00. In addition, the five employees are booked on a skydiving experience for £235.00 per person. What will be the total cost for each employee?

Answer:

Short-answer questions

Specific instructions to students

- The following questions will help you understand decimal places, mean, mode, median, range (interpreting statistics), probability format, style and data handling.
- Read the following questions, then answer accordingly.
- You need to show all working, you can use the blank Notes pages at the back of this book.

The following questions relate to Morestores Ltd, a retail organization that sells a wide range of products, mainly catalogue surplus stock.

QUESTION 1

Morestores Ltd has included this diagram in its staff handbook, to show the staff structure. The next few questions are related to this diagram.

a What is this type of diagram called?

Answer:

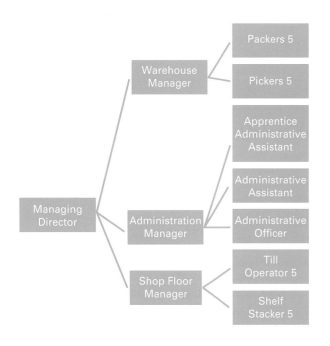

b How many members of staff is the Shop Floor Manager responsible for?

Answer:

c How many members of staff report directly to the Managing Director?

Answer:

d How many members of staff, including the Managing Director, work at Morestores Ltd?

Answer:

QUESTION 2

The next few questions relate to the holiday entitlements and attendance bonus scheme, provided below, as they appear in the staff handbook at Morestores Ltd.

Number of years in service	Annual holiday entitlement	❖ Additional holiday for 100% attendance
Less than 1 year	10 days (pro rata)	N/A
1 – 3 years	15 days	0.5 day
4 – 6 years	20 days	1 day
7 – 9 years	25 days	1.5 days
Over 10 years	30 days	2 days

❖ *This additional holiday bonus is only applied in the year following a 100% attendance record*

a How have the details of the holiday entitlement been presented?

Answer:

b What is the maximum annual holiday entitlement at Morestores Ltd, without taking any available additional holiday bonus into account?

Answer:

c If a member of staff has worked at Morestores Ltd for 8 years, how many days holiday are they entitled to?

Answer:

_____

d True or false? The holiday entitlements table provided contains 3 rows and 5 columns.

Answer:

_____

e How much additional time off would a member of staff receive if they had a 100% attendance record in the previous year and had worked for Morestores Ltd for 11 years?

Answer:

_____

f If a member of staff had a total holiday entitlement of 20 days and 1 day attendance bonus, how long would they have worked at Morestores Ltd?

Answer:

_____

g What would the total holiday entitlement, including attendance bonus, for a member of staff who had 100% attendance record in their previous year and had worked at Morestores Ltd for 8 years?

Answer:

_____

QUESTION 3

With reference to Morestores Ltd, a retail organization that sells a wide range of products, mainly catalogue surplus stock.

The next few questions relate to the staff handbook that all new members of staff at Morestores Ltd receive upon starting their employment.

a The staff handbook is designed to do which of the following?

   (1) Persuade

   (2) Advise

   (3) Instruct

   (4) Convince

Answer:

_____

b The first page of the staff handbook contains a welcome message from the Managing Director. How would this message be most likely to be presented?

   (1) In memo format

   (2) In charts and graphs

   (3) In paragraphs

   (4) In bullet points

Answer:

_____

c The staff handbook contains information about actions to take in the case of emergencies, such as discovering a fire in the workplace. This information would be best presented in which of the following forms?

   (1) Flow chart

   (2) Pie chart

   (3) Table

   (4) Line graph

Answer:

_____

d Assuming that all new employees receive basic training on how to tackle small fires in the workplace, how would it be best to illustrate the use of firefighting equipment in the staff handbook?

   (1) Using signs

   (2) Using diagrams

   (3) Using bar charts

   (4) Using tables

Answer:

_____

e The staff handbook also includes a Sales Report of retail products over the previous year. The sales achieved in each quarter are displayed in the diagram on the next page. The next few questions relate to this Sales Report.

Morestores Ltd – Quarterly Sales Report

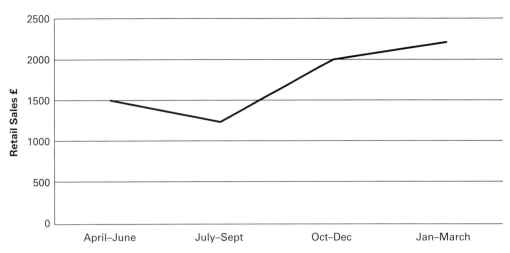

f How has the information been presented in the Sales Report diagram?

Answer:

_____

g In the Sales Report, during which quarter did Morestores Ltd have its highest sales?

Answer:

_____

h According to the Sales Report, which quarter did Morestores Ltd have its biggest sales increase?

Answer:

_____

QUESTION 4

Petra Bolton is the Managing Director of Morestores Ltd. She has been told by a catalogue company that if she spends an average of £1000 per month over a 12 month period, then they will give her a reward card. This reward card allows her to have a 2% discount off monthly totals over £1000 spent, or 5% off spends above £2000.

Over one year the company spends the following amounts:

Jan	Feb	March	April
£875.89	£917.52	£1007.85	£2158
May	**June**	**July**	**Aug**
£1103.57	£1012.50	£1000.02	£506
Sep	**Oct**	**Nov**	**Dec**
£905.78	£1010.12	£974.58	£751.29

a What is the range of Petra's spending?

Answer:

_____

a In which month does she spend the least? Why do you think that is?

Answer:

_____

_____

_____

c Does Petra qualify for a reward card? Show your working.

Answer:

_____

_____

_____

d Calculate the savings Petra could have made each qualifying month if she had already had a reward card.

Answer:

_____

_____

_____

_____

e What is the total amount she could have saved?

Answer:

_____

_____

QUESTION 5

The next few questions relate to a local retail organization. The retail organization has had three pupils, aged 14 and 15, that have attended for work experience, as part of an arrangement with a local school. They have worked really well over the last 3 months and have fitted into the team of 5 till operators extremely well. As a reward and a team-bonding exercise, the Shop Floor Manager decides to ask the Warehouse Manager and his team to look after the Shop Floor on a Wednesday afternoon and takes her team out to a 'Handmade Chocolate Making' workshop. She gains parental permission, via the school, to include the three pupils in the outing.

This table shows the course prices to the chocolate making workshop.

	1 March – 21 March 29 Sept – 13 Nov £	22 March – 12 July 21 Aug – 28 Sept £	13 July – 20 Aug £
Adult	15	21	24
Child (10–15)	7	12	14

a How much will it cost the manager to take the work experience pupils, the whole team and herself, to the workshop on 15 March?

Answer:

_____

b The chocolate making workshop also operates a retail outlet that sells handmade chocolates to the public. It opens 4 days a week. This table shows the days and the expected number of people to visit each day. The Workshop estimates that usually on a Wednesday, 40% of the customers buy Truffle selection packs. How many Truffle selection packs must they make sure to stock?

Monday	Wednesday	Friday	Saturday
150	90	225	250

Answer:

_____

c The chocolate making workshop records the number of customers that visit the retail outlet on a Saturday. The chart shows the results.

Number of customers visiting the retail outlet per hour

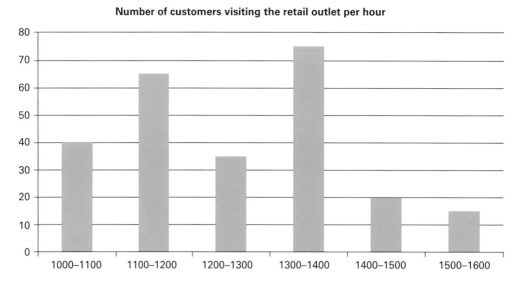

During which period did the greatest number of customers visit the retail outlet?

Answer

QUESTION 6

Extract and interpret data from a table

The Old Hall Hotel keeps records for several years. This table shows the room occupancy rates for the last five years. They show the percentage of rooms that were occupied each month.

a   Calculate the average (mean) percentage room occupancy for each year and insert your answers in the table.

Percentage room occupancy 2008–2012					
	2008	2009	2010	2011	2012
January	22	23	24	26	26
February	29	30	31	31	32
March	38	39	41	41	42
April	45	47	49	48	49
May	65	66	67	67	69
June	70	73	76	76	77
July	65	69	71	71	73
August	76	79	82	83	84
September	77	78	82	84	85
October	51	53	54	54	56
November	30	31	32	33	34
December	30	30	31	32	32

Average percentage room occupancy for each year					
Year	2008	2009	2010	2011	2012
Mean					

b   Present this data as a bar chart using the squared paper below. Then calculate the range of percentage room occupancy for each year.

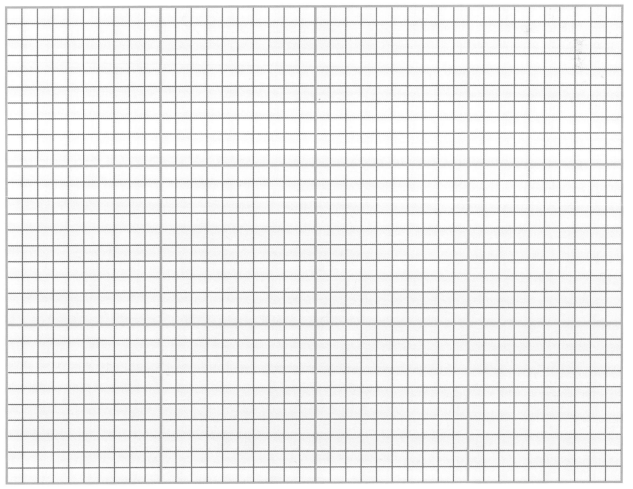

Range of percentage room occupancy for each year					
Year	2008	2009	2010	2011	2012
Range					

c Present the percentage room occupancy data for the year 2010 as a line graph. Put the months of the year on the horizontal axis and the percentage occupancy up the vertical axis.

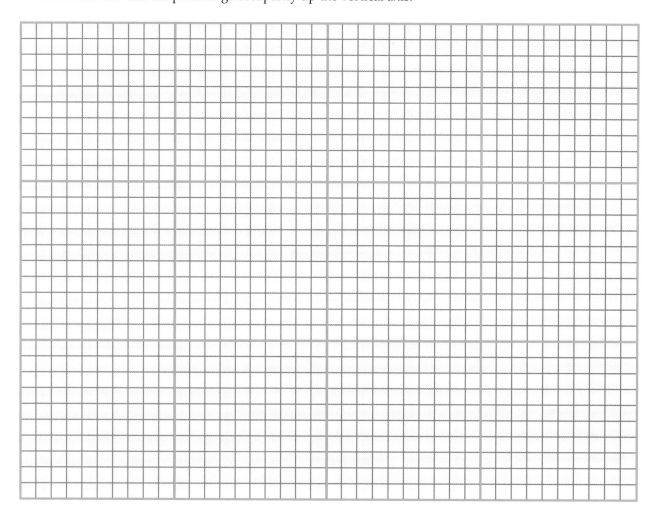

Unit 19:
Practice Written Exam for Retail

Section A: English
Section B: Mathematics

QUESTION and ANSWER BOOK

Section	Topic	Number of questions	Marks
A	English	16	119
B	Mathematics	14	130
		Total 30	Total 249

The sections may be completed in the order of your choice.

Speaking, listening and communication

Task 1: Informal discussion

12 marks

You are organizing a party to celebrate raising £1 million. This event will be **advertised** as the 'One Million Party'. Your manager has asked you and your friends to plan three **money**-raising **activities**.

<table>
<tr><td>

Chairperson

Your role is to lead and control the meeting. You must manage time, encourage discussion, deal with any disagreements and write down any plans and arrangements.

You need to set tasks for members in the group.

</td><td>

Alex

Your role is to carry out research in to raffle activities. You need to share and discuss your ideas with others in the group.

</td></tr>
<tr><td>

Sam

Your role is to carry out research in to quiz activities. You need to share and discuss your ideas with others in the group

</td><td>

Ali

Your role is to carry out research in to karaoke activities. You need to share and discuss your ideas with others in the group.

</td></tr>
</table>

Task 2: Formal meeting

15 marks

You have shared ideas for fund-raising activities to take place at the 'One Million Party'. You meet to have a formal meeting with your manager to discuss the ideas, the planning and and support you will need.

You will be marked on:

- preparation for the discussion

- making relevant and detailed contributions to the discussion

- responding appropriately to other people

- presenting information and your own point of view clearly to others

- making different types of contributions to the discussion

- using appropriate language.

Task 3: Discussion (15 minutes) 12 marks

You are organizing a party to celebrate raising £1 million. This event will be advertised as the 'One Million Pound Party'. One of the senior managers at the charity has asked you and some colleagues to plan money-raising activities for all ticket holders on the night. He/she feels this will make the event more exciting.

Chairperson	**Alex**
Your role is to lead and control the meeting. You must manage time, encourage discussion, deal with any disagreements and write down any plans and arrangements. You need to set tasks for members in the group.	Your role is to carry out research in to raffle activities. You need to share and discuss your ideas with others in the group.

Sam	**Ali**
Your role is to carry out research into quiz activities. You need to share and discuss your ideas with others in the group.	Your role is to carry out research into karaoke activities. You need to share and discuss your ideas with others in the group.

Les
Your role is to carry out research into general fundraising ideas /activities. You need to share and discuss your ideas with others in the group.

Task 4: Speaking and listening (15 minutes) 15 marks

Senior managers need to be informed and about the plans for the celebration. You need to present the information persuasively to one senior manager (this could be the tutor in role).

Learners need to consider what support they will use:

Microsoft Office PowerPoint	Cue-cards	Images
Physical resources	Research summary	Presentation plan (introduction, middle, end)
Projector	Interactive whiteboard	Flip chart

You will be marked on:

- preparation for the discussion

- making relevant and detailed contributions to the discussion

- responding appropriately to other people

- presenting information and your own point of view clearly to others

- making different types of contributions to the discussion

- using appropriate language

- presenting relevant information and ideas clearly

- presenting where appropriately, persuasively to others

- adapting your presentation to suit the audience, purpose and situation

- using visual aids, if appropriate, to make an effective presentation.

Reading 🔢
Organizing a Party

You and your Manager (Mr Mahmood) are organizing a party for you store's 50th birthday. Your manager would like you to consider using last year's Christmas party venue. He gives you a promotion article from a magazine about a party venue (Document 1) and a letter from a previous party planner (Document 2).

You have **45 minutes** to read the documents and answer the questions below. You should spend about **5–10 minutes** of this time reading the documents.

Document 1:

Promotional Article

Eastside Hotel Review

By Jane Summer

This is an attractive and pleasant venue for a party. What a fabulous experience I had last Saturday at Eastside, where I held my own birthday party! It has a warm, friendly and welcoming atmosphere with outstanding hospitality.

IT'S DIFFERENT!
I feel there is something quite special about Eastside. It is really very different. It's fresh and unstuffy. It is so very modern, and oozes glamour and style. It makes you feel like a celebrity!

FOOD AND DRINKS
The food was excellent and they offer free drinks to all party guests for the first hour.

OVERNIGHT STAY
I really indulged myself and stayed over after the party in a luxurious room that was really quite inexpensive. The accommodation is really good value for money.

LOCATION
Eastside set in 10 acres of beautiful landscaped gardens and is the nearest hotel to Parker's House, recently voted Britain's finest stately home. Guests even get a free pass for Parker's House as a special incentive!

My verdict: 10/10

To find out more visit their webpage:
www.eastside.com
or telephone: 0546 3456540

Document 2:

Mr R Mahmood
Bent's Retail Outlet
29 Newton Road
London
LW2 3KL

Dear Mr Mahmood

I am pleased to hear that your organization's 50th Birthday party will take place this year. I feel it is important that we hold the party because it will make staff feel appreciated. Additionally, it will encourage staff to continue to work successfully within your retail outlet. However, I have been told that Eastside is being considered as a possible venue for the event.

As you are aware, I organized a Christmas party at Eastside on behalf of Bent's Retail Outlet. This event turned out to be very expensive and the staff was rather unhelpful and unfriendly. Unfortunately, the choice of food was poor, as there were only two options for each course. There were 100 people at the party and only five members of staff so service was very slow and the food was cold.

On a brighter note, their disco was absolutely excellent. The DJ was very entertaining and played pop music all night. The dance floor was always full. He also had some really good games to break things up a bit.

There is limited accommodation and people were disappointed that they could not stay over as it was fully booked.

I think that most people would prefer the party not to take place at Eastside.

Yours sincerely
Su Win

Answer all the questions using information from the documents. You do not need to write in sentences.

QUESTION 1   2 marks

Give two reasons why Su Win feels it is important to hold a party.

Answer:

_____

_____

QUESTION 2   1 mark

According to Document 2, what type of music did the DJ play at the party last year?

(1) House music
(2) Dance music
(3) Pop music
(4) Reggae music

Answer:

_____

QUESTION 3   4 marks

Give four reasons why Su Win does not recommend Eastside.

Answer:

_____

_____

_____

_____

QUESTION 4   5 marks

Name five things Jane Summer likes about Eastside.

Answer:

_____

_____

_____

_____

_____

_____

_____

QUESTION 5   2 marks

What could you do if you need to find out anything else about Eastside?

Answer:

_____

_____

QUESTION 6   4 marks

a   Do you think Eastside would be a good venue for the party?

Answer:

_____

b   Explain the reasons for your choice

Answer:

_____

QUESTION 7   2 marks

Using a dictionary – explain the word *oozes*.

Answer:

_____

_____

_____

QUESTION 8   2 marks

Using a dictionary – explain the word *indulge*.

Answer:

_____

_____

_____

QUESTION 9   3 marks

In Document 1, how does Jane Summer encourage you to book a party at Eastside?

Answer:

_____

_____

_____

_____

_____

Writing  L1

- This task assesses your writing skills.
- Remember to write in sentences, using accurate spelling, punctuation and grammar. Allow time to check your work.
- Remember that spelling, punctuation and grammar will be assessed.

BARNTON WATER PARK

Open 7 days a week

We need a number of
full-time and part-time staff
to work in our busy gift shops.

Must be enthusiastic and able to work as part of a team.

Interested? Please send a letter of application to the manager:
David Brownley, Barnton Water Park,
Runcorn Lane, High Legh WA11 5LB.

Please state your availability for work. Give details of skills and any previous experience.

QUESTION 1   **15 marks**

You find the above job advert in your local newspaper and decide to apply.

On a separate sheet of paper, write a letter of application to the manager of Barnton Water Park.

In your letter you should include:

- Where you saw the job advertised
- Details about yourself and your skills
- Previous experience or qualifications
- Your availability for work

You should:

- Use correct letter format
- Write in full sentences
- Use correct spelling, punctuation and grammar

Remember to write in sentences, using accurate spelling, punctuation and grammar. Plan your answer before you write your draft and final letter.

You should spend approximately 20 minutes writing this letter.

Writing ⓛ2

- There are two tasks which assess your writing skills.
- For both tasks, remember to write in sentences, using accurate spelling, punctuation and grammar. Allow time to check your work.
- Remember that spelling, punctuation and grammar will be assessed in both tasks.

QUESTION 1   10 marks

You are organizing a party with a few colleagues to celebrate having raised £1 million pounds. This party will be called the 'One Million Pound Party'. On a separate sheet of paper, write an email to all the staff at Charity Ten to tell them what you are planning. You have organized a venue, some activities, food and drinks. You need to persuade the staff to attend the party and say why it will be successful. The email address is allstaff@charityten.co.uk

QUESTION 2   15 marks

You and some colleagues are organizing the 'One Million Pound Party'. The senior manager likes your ideas but has asked you to consider two venues. He has given you a local magazine article/promotional piece about a party venue (Document 1), a letter from a previous party organizer (Document 2) and emails from employees (Document 3). Read the following documents, then write a formal letter back to the senior manager to tell him about your choice of venue and reasons why, using an appropriate format. Plan your answer before you write your draft and final letter. The Senior Manager's address is:

Mr R Stapleton
Charity Ten Office House
37 Gable Rise
London
SE7 4NW

Document 1:

Promotional Article

Eastside Hotel Review

By Jane Summer

This is an attractive and pleasant venue for a party. What a fabulous experience I had last Saturday at Eastside, where I held my own birthday party! It has a warm, friendly and welcoming atmosphere with outstanding hospitality.

IT'S DIFFERENT!

I feel there is something quite special about Eastside. It is really very different. It's fresh and unstuffy. It is so very modern, and oozes glamour and style. It makes you feel like a celebrity!

FOOD AND DRINKS

The food was excellent and they offer free drinks to all party guests for the first hour.

OVERNIGHT STAY

I really indulged myself and stayed over after the party in a luxurious room that was really quite inexpensive. The accommodation is really good value for money.

LOCATION

Eastside set in 10 acres of beautiful landscaped gardens and is the nearest hotel to Parker's House, recently voted Britain's finest stately home. Guests even get a free pass for Parker's House as a special incentive!

My verdict: 10/10

Document 2:

22 Market Street
Burlington
B11 9HL

Mr R Stapleton
Charity Ten Office House
37 Gable Rise
London
SE7 4NW

Dear Mr Mahmood

RE: Fund raising party event 2013

As you are aware, I organized the above event on behalf of Charity Ten in January of this year. I feel it would be most helpful if I provided you with feedback to help you in planning future events.

The party took place at Bongos, and this was relatively cheap and the staff were extremely friendly. It is a very traditional place with traditional English food. Unfortunately, the choice of food was poor, as there were only two options for each course. There were 100 people at the party and only 5 members of staff so service was very slow and the food was cold. They do offer a buffet party package which would have improved the event tremendously.

Their disco was absolutely excellent. The DJ was very entertaining and played popular music all night. The dance floor was always full. He also had some really good games to break things up a bit.

Unfortunately, Bongos does not have any accommodation and people were disappointed that they could not stay over.

My colleague, Paula, has mentioned that Eastside is being considered for the Million Pound Party. She has been to an event there recently with her husband and she says it has a very modern day feel about it with light and airy spaces. She does not want to feel old and says that Eastside makes you feel young and lively.

Another colleague mentioned that he thought it would be a good idea to go to Eastside as the food is very good. He also suggested that a fancy dress theme would be good as this would make it much more fun, with a prize for the best costume.

I think most people would like the party to take place at Eastside.

Yours sincerely,

Rajesh Kapoor

Deputy Fundraising Manager

Document 3:

To: r.stapleton@charityten.co.uk

From: j.key@charityten.co.uk

Subject: Million Pound Party

Roger,

I have recently heard that Eastside may be booked for the million pound party. I would like to comment that when we went to the party at Bongos my colleagues and I had an excellent night. We had a good choice of food and the service was really fast. Their DJ is very good, with fabulous music and he even arranged for us to do some Karaoke. I would very much plead with you to book Bongos again this time; otherwise I am afraid I do not think I would want to go to the million pound party.

Thanks,

Jon

To: r.stapleton@charityten.co.uk

From: m.lax@charityten.co.uk

Subject: Million Pound Party

Roger,

I have heard that Eastside is being considered as a possible venue for the forthcoming party. I went there last year and my friends and I thought the venue was not ideal. The food was very 'new cuisine' with ungenerous servings and the service was poor, the venue was unpleasant and the drinks were very expensive. The venue generally was too fashionable in my eyes with too many modern paintings on the walls. We need a party at a venue with a more traditional feel and if the party is to be held at Eastside then I will not be purchasing a ticket. I beg you to consider this viewpoint.

Cheers,

Max

To: r.stapleton@charityten.co.uk

From: j.ronksley@charityten.co.uk

Subject: Million Pound Party

Roger,

Les has mentioned that the million pound party may be arranged at Eastside. This would be not be good venue. I was disappointed when we last went there because the car park is so far from the party room. People do not like to walk a long distance from the car. This really spoilt the night for me and my family. Can you please make sure we book Bongos for the million pound party as they have car parking directly outside the party room?

Many thanks,

Julie

Write your letter on a separate sheet of paper.

Section B: Mathematics

- You should give details of your method of solution when appropriate.
- Unless stated, diagrams are not drawn to scale.
- Scale drawing solutions will not be acceptable where you are asked to calculate.

Test 1 🔵

QUESTION 1   6 marks

Amir, Bethany, Clive and Davina were the finalists in a quiz competition. In the final there were five rounds with ten questions for each competitor in each round. They gained one point for each correct answer.

After **three** rounds the positions and scores were as follows.

Position	Name	Score
1	Bethany	24
2	Davina	23
3	Amir	20
4	Clive	19

In **Round 4**, Amir answered 8 questions correctly, Bethany answered 5 questions correctly, Clive answered 8 questions correctly and Davina answered 9 questions correctly.

In **Round 5**, Amir answered all 10 questions correctly and the other three each answered 7 of their questions correctly.

Complete the final table after all **five** rounds showing the position and score for each competitor.

Position	Name	Score
1		
2		
3		
4		

Who would have been the winner if the points gained in the last round (Round 5) were doubled?

Answer:

_____

QUESTION 2   15 marks

Your youth club arrange an entertainment evening at the community hall.

You have been asked to present a report on how much money was spent (Costs), how much money was collected (Income) and the profit made on the event.

You have the following information.

- The hall was hired for 4 hours at a cost of £25 per hour.
- 200 tickets were printed at a cost using the formula **Cost = Fixed cost of £10 + £5 for every 50 tickets**.
- Cost of food for making refreshments was £120.
- The band's fee was £250.
- 160 tickets were sold at £3 each.
- On average, the 160 people who attended the event spent £2.50 each on refreshments.

Remember to present your report clearly.

Answer:

QUESTION 3   9 marks

The diagram below is a scale drawing showing the positions of 4 points *A*, *B*, *P* and *Q* on level ground.

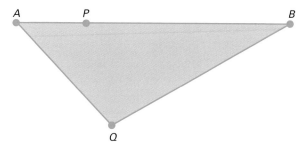

Scale: 1 cm represents 1 km

There are 2 possible routes to walk from *A* to *B*. You can walk from *A* to *P* to *B*, or you can walk from *A* to *Q* to *B*.

The different walking conditions between the points means that your average speed would be 4 km per hour between *A* and *P*, 6 km per hour between *P* and *B*, and 5 km per hour along the whole route from *A* through *Q* to *B*.

Using the scale drawing, calculate which of the two routes would be the quicker and by how much.

Answer:

QUESTION 4   11 marks

A supermarket sells a brand of tinned salmon in tins of two sizes.

It states on all tins that for health reasons the salmon must be eaten within two days of the tin being opened.

What is the price charged per 10 grams of salmon for each tin?

Answer:

_____

_____

Why would someone buy two small tins rather than one big tin?

Answer:

Bags containing 10 tangerines are sold at the supermarket for £1.20. A special offer advertises

Buy 2 bags for £2

Alex buys just the one bag. Liam buys two bags on the special offer.

During the following week Alex ate all of her tangerines, but Liam only ate 16 of his tangerines, as the other four had gone bad.

By calculating the price of a single tangerine eaten by Alex and the price of a single tangerine eaten by Liam, who do you think had the better deal?

Answer:

QUESTION 5   12 marks

The table below gives 3 measurements, both in gallons and litres.

Gallons	4	15	20
Litres	18	68	91

On the graph paper below, use the data in the table to draw a conversion graph between gallons and litres.

Use your graph to find an estimate for,

7 gallons in litres,

Answer:

_____

50 litres in gallons,

Answer:

_____

450 litres in gallons.

Answer:

_____

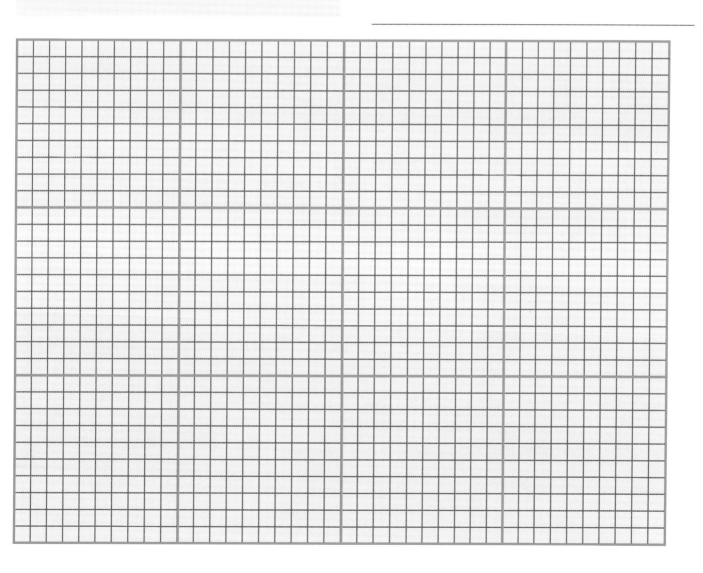

QUESTION 6   7 marks

In a hockey league, teams are awarded 3 points for a win, 1 point for a draw and 0 points if they lose a match.

A team called Burnhill Sticks is top of the league and has won 12 games, drawn 4 and lost 2. How many points does the team have?

Answer:

_____

Four other teams in the league have 29 points each.

These four teams have all won a **different** number of matches.

Complete the table below to show **four** possible ways of gaining 29 points after playing 18 games.

Played	Won	Drawn	Lost	Points
18				29
18				29
18				29
18				29

For working:

QUESTION 7   5 marks

A shop on the High Street displays the following sign:

SALE

20% OFF
When you spend
£25 or more

You have £22.

How many boxes of chocolates priced at £5 each can you afford to buy?

You must show all your calculations in order to explain your answer.

Answer:

Test 2

QUESTION 1   6 marks

Eight competitors run in a race at an athletics meeting.

The name and the time for each competitor are shown in the table below.

Complete the POSITION column to show the position of each competitor.

NAME	TIME	POSITION
Khan	2 min 10 sec	
Allen	1 min 42 sec	1st
Cooper	2 min 00 sec	
Peters	1 min 47 sec	2nd
Wong	1 min 55 sec	5th
Durman	2 min 04 sec	7th
Hooton	1 min 50 sec	
Selby	1 min 54 sec	

In how many seconds under two minutes did Allen complete the race?

Answer:

_____

Which two competitors finished closest together?

Answer:

_____

QUESTION 2   6 marks

The top of the medal table at the 2012 Olympic Games in London was

COUNTRY	GOLD	SILVER	BRONZE
1. U.S.A.	46	29	29
2. China	38	27	23
3. Great Britain	29	17	19
4. Russia	24	26	32
5. South Korea	13	8	7

What was the total number of medals won by the Great Britain team?

Answer:

Find the total number of gold medals won by these five countries.

Answer:

If 3 points were awarded for a gold, 2 points for a silver and 1 point for a bronze, by how many points would Russia be ahead of Great Britain?

Answer:

QUESTION 3   **6 marks**

Harry decides to visit his friend who lives 24 miles away. He is unsure about whether to call a taxi, use the local bus service or cycle to his friend's house.

His friend will give him a lift back home so he does not have to worry about the return journey.

TAXI

£2.50 + £1.25 per mile

Journey time
½ hour

BUS (every hour)

Fare £5.36

Journey time
55 minutes

CYCLE

Average Speed
12 miles per hour

Compare the costs and the times taken for the three methods of travel, showing all your calculations.

Which method of travel would you recommend Harry to choose?

Give one advantage and one disadvantage of your recommendation.

Answer:

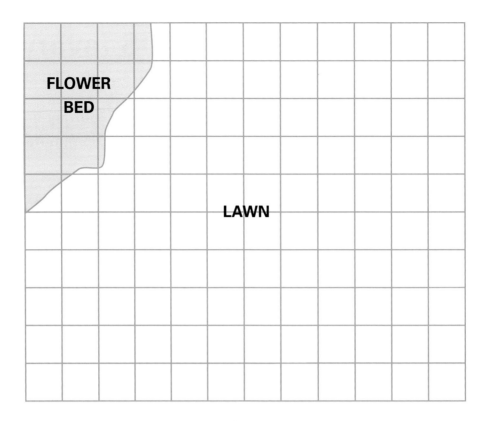

FLOWER BED

LAWN

QUESTION 4   14 marks

The garden of a house is a rectangle 12 metres long and 10 metres wide.

Calculate the area of this garden, clearly stating the units used.

Answer:

The scale diagram above, drawn on a centimetre square grid, shows the garden with a flower bed in one corner. The rest of the garden is a lawn.

Estimate the area of the lawn.

Answer:

The garden is to be fenced along the two long sides and along one of the short sides.

Posts are to be placed at 2m intervals along these three sides.

Corner and end posts cost £3.50 each and the other posts cost £2 each.

What will be the total cost for all the posts required?

Answer:

A restaurant has the following menu for its customers.

Moorfield restaurant

Today's *MENU*

Starters

Soup of the Day	£3.50
Melon	£4.25
Thai Fishcakes	£4.75

Main Course

Cod and Chips	£7.50
Lamb Shank	£8.75
Trout	£11.50
Sirloin Steak	£13.25

Dessert

Ice Cream	£3.00
Apple Pie	£4.25
Lemon Cheesecake	£4.50
Summer Pudding	£4.75

Tea or coffee	£1.75

Four friends Ann, Sunita, Bryn and Declan have been eating at the restaurant.

As a starter Ann had soup and the other three all had melon.

For the main course Ann and Sunita had trout, Bryn had lamb shank and Declan had sirloin steak.

Bryn had apple pie for dessert and the other three had summer pudding.

All except Ann had tea or coffee.

Complete the following bill showing the amount spent on each course and the total amount spent.

	£
Starters	
Main Courses	
Desserts	
Tea or Coffee	
TOTAL	

For working:

They decided to divide the bill equally between them.

Would it have cost more or less for Ann, if they had each paid for their own meal?

What was the difference?

Answer:

QUESTION 6   6 marks

The plan of a bedroom is shown on the grid below.

Scale: 1 cm represents 50 cm.

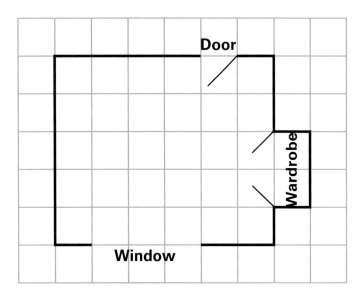

You need to position a bed and a dressing table in the bedroom.

The bed is 2 metres long and 1 metre wide.

The dressing table is 150 cm long and 50 cm wide.

Using the scale given, show where you think is the best place to position the bed and the dressing table.

QUESTION 7   16 marks

Angela Rain's time-sheet at her work place for the week beginning 16 March 2013 is shown below.

Some of the entries are not shown.

Fill in these spaces with the correct numbers.

Angela is paid £7.50 per hour between Monday and Friday.

On a Saturday she is paid £12 per hour for working up to 1 pm.

Calculate Angela's wage for the week shown.

Answer:

Any work done after 1 pm on a Saturday earns double the Saturday morning hourly rate.

Can she make up her wage to be at least £400 by working on Saturday afternoon, bearing in mind that she has to leave her work place by 3.30pm?

Show all of your working.

Answer:

NAME: Angela Rain			WEEK BEGINNING: 16-03-2013		
	Start	End	Hours	Lunch	Hours Worked
Monday	08.00	17.30	9½	1	8½
Tuesday	08.00	17.00		1	
Wednesday	08.30		8	½	
Thursday		17.00	9	½	8½
Friday	07.30	16.30	9		7½
Saturday	08.00	13.00	5	0	5

For working:

Retail Glossary

Advertising   The activity of producing advertisements for commercial products or services.

Annual holiday entitlement   The number of days an employee is allowed to take off work (as holiday).

Appointment   An arrangement to meet someone at an office or business at a particular time.

Apprenticeship   A framework consisting of an NVQ, functional skills qualification and a technical certificate. Learning takes place both in the workplace and with a learning provider.

Bank manager   The manager of a branch office of a bank.

Barista   Someone who makes and serves coffee in a coffee bar.

Billboard advertising   An advertisement on a huge board placed by the side of a road.

Business growth   Any organization whose business generates significant cash flows or earnings, which increase at significantly faster rates than the overall economy.

Butchering knife   A heavy-duty knife with a broad, sharp blade for cutting meat.

Competitive   Able to compete with other similar products, by being equally or better priced, or providing an equally good service.

Complaint   A statement that something is unsatisfactory or unacceptable.

Computer   A machine that stores programs and information in electronic form and can be used for a variety of processes, for example, writing, calculating and communicating on the Internet.

Cordless mouse   A mouse with no cord that transmits infrared or radio signals (RF) to a base station receiver.

Covering letter   A letter sent with your Curriculum Vitae or Application Form to provide additional information on your skills and experience.

Curriculum Vitae   A written description of your work experience, educational background and skills.

Customer Care Policy   A set of rules for how employees should deal with customers at a business.

Customer loyalty   The idea of making your customers want to always come back to your business to buy more goods or services.

Customer satisfaction   A measure of how happy customers are with the goods or services of an organization, as measured by the number of repeat customers.

Customer service department   A department which deals with customers and their complaints and orders.

Deli counter   A counter that provides a variety of cold meats, cheeses, salads and over the counter food items.

Department store   A large store that sells many varieties of goods in different departments.

Direct mail advertising   Using the postal service to send an advertising message, which could be in the form of a brochure.

Discount   Deduct an amount from the usual price of something.

Flow chart   A graphic representation of a process, such as a manufacturing operation, indicating the various steps taken as the product moves along the production line.

Formal letter   A business letter written in formal language, usually when writing from one business organization to another.

Graph   A graph is an image that represents data symbolically and is used to present complex information and numerical data in a simple, compact format.

Holiday insurance   An insurance product designed to cover the costs of unexpected events during a holiday.

Internet advertising   Also known as online advertising, where promotional messages appear on a website that you're visiting.

Invoice   A list of goods sent or services provided that is sent to a customer that need to be paid (like a bill).

Letter   A written or printed communication addressed to a person or organization and usually sent by post.

Letter of complaint   A persuasive letter sent by a customer to an organization to express dissatisfaction with a product or service.

Managing Director   The person with the most senior position in an organization and with the responsibility of managing it all.

Market research   The gathering and evaluation of data regarding consumers' preferences for products and services.

Microsoft Office   Brand name of a suite of computer programs for Windows and Mac, including Word, Excel, PowerPoint.

Mobile shop   A large vehicle that has been changed into a shop and is driven from place to place.

Online retailer   A business or person that sells goods to the consumer via the Internet.

Overtime   The amount of time someone works beyond normal working hours.

Patisserie   A shop where French pastries and cakes are sold.

Personal shopper   Someone who helps others shop by giving advice and making suggestions to customers.

Pie chart   A circular chart divided into sectors; each sector shows the relative size of each value.

Purchase order   A document authorizing a seller to deliver goods, with payments to be made at a later date.

Retail   A business or person that sells goods to the consumer.

Retail assistant   A person who arranges stock and helps customers.

Retail outlet   A store that sells smaller quantities of products or services to the general public.

Sales   A quantity or amount sold.

Sales promotion   A marketing technique designed to create sales for a product over a defined period of time.

Shelf stacker   A person whose job it is to fill the shelves and displays in a supermarket or other shops with goods for sale.

Shop assistant   A salesperson in a store.

Shopping centre   A purpose-built complex of shops and restaurants.

Staff handbook   A document that provides guidance about company policies and procedures for employees.

Starter   A dish served before the main meal.

Stock   The goods or merchandise kept on the premises of a business or warehouse available for sale or distribution.

Stock control   The process of making sure that the correct level of stock is maintained.

Stocktake   To count the goods and materials owned by an organization or available for sale in a shop at a particular time.

Supermarket   A large self-service store selling foods and household goods.

Surplus stock   Having more of a product than is needed.

Till operator   A person whose job it is to operate the till, often employed by a supermarket.

Timesheet   A piece of paper for recording the number of hours worked.

Training course   Instruction to teach new work skills.

White goods   Large appliances, such as fridges or cookers.

Wholesale   The sale of goods in large quantities, as for resale by a retailer.

English Glossary

Adjective   A type of word that describes NOUNS (things, people and places), for example *sharp*, *warm* or *handsome*.

Adverb   A type of word that describes VERBS (things happening), for example *slowly*, *often* or *quickly*.

Apostrophe   A PUNCTUATION mark with two main functions: (1) shows where letters have been missed out when words or phrases are shortened, for example changing *cannot* to *can't*, or *I will* to *I'll*; (2) shows where a NOUN 'possesses' something, for example *Dave's bike*, *the cat's whiskers* or *St John's Wood*.

Capital letter   Used to begin a SENTENCE, to begin the names of people, days, months and places, and for abbreviations such as *RSPCA* or *FBI*.

Comma   A PUNCTUATION mark that has many uses, usually to separate phrases in a long SENTENCE so that it is easier to read and understand, or to separate items in a list.

Formal language   The type of language used when speaking to or writing to someone you don't know, such as your bank manager (e.g. 'I am writing to request a bank statement').

Full stop   A PUNCTUATION mark used at the end of SENTENCES.

Future tense   The VERB forms we use to talk about things that will happen in future (e.g. 'I *will watch* television tonight').

Homophone   A word that sounds the same as another word, but has a different spelling and meaning, for example *break* and *brake*.

Informal language   The type of language used when you are speaking to or writing to someone you know well, such as a friend (e.g. 'Hi, how are you? Do you fancy coming to the cinema with me?').

Instructions   A series or list of statements designed to show someone how to do something, for example to use some equipment or to follow some rules.

Noun   A word used to refer to a thing, person or place, for example *chair*, *George* or *Sheffield*.

Paragraph   A section of writing about the same subject or topic, that begins on a new line and consists of one or more SENTENCES.

Past tense   The VERB forms we use to talk about things that have happened in the past (e.g. 'I *watched* television last night').

Present tense   The VERB forms we use to talk about things that are happening now (e.g. 'I *am watching* television').

Pronouns   Words that are used instead of NOUNS (things, people and places), for example *he*, *she*, *we*, *it*, *who*, *something*, *ourselves*.

Punctuation   Marks used in writing to help make it clear and organized, by separating or joining together words or phrases, or by adding or changing emphasis.

Question mark   A PUNCTUATION mark used at the end of a question, to show that you have asked something.

Sentence   A group of words, beginning with a CAPITAL LETTER and ending with a FULL STOP, QUESTION MARK or exclamation mark, put together using correct grammar, to make a meaningful statement or question, etc.

Verb   Word used to indicate an action, for example *mix*, *smile* or *walk*.

Mathematics Glossary

Actual The exact calculation of a set of numbers.

Analogue clock A clock that displays minute and hour hands and shows the time changing continuously.

Area The size of a surface; the amount of space in a two-dimensional shape or property, e.g. the floor space of a room or flat.

Decimal A way of organizing numbers based around the number ten (the most familiar system used in the world today).

Decimal point A mark, often a full stop, used in a number to divide between whole numbers and FRACTIONS of whole numbers shown in DECIMAL form.

Digital clock A clock that tells the time using numbers instead of hands and shows the time changing digitally – from one exact value to the next.

Estimate (1) A calculation that requires a rough guess rather than working out the actual figure; (2) to work out this value.

Fraction A quantity or amount that is not a whole number, e.g. less than 1. A part of a whole number.

Imperial The British system of units for weights and measures before the METRIC system, including pounds, stones, miles, feet and inches.

Mean A form of average of a set of numbers. To calculate the mean, add all of the numbers together and then divide by how many numbers there are.

Median A form of average of a set of numbers. To calculate the median, place the numbers in numerical order and then find the middle number.

Metric An international DECIMAL system of units for weights and measures, including kilograms, grams, kilometres, metres and centimetres.

Mode A form of average of a set of numbers. To calculate the mode, look for the number that appears most often.

Percentage A proportion, or FRACTION, that means part of one hundred.

Perimeter The total lengths of all of the sides of a two-dimensional shape or AREA, e.g. the distance around the outside of a room.

Range The difference between the largest and smallest numbers in a set of figures.

Ratio A way to compare the amounts of things – how much of one thing there is compared to how much of another thing.

Scales An instrument used to measure the weight of an object or person.

Volume The amount of three-dimensional space that an object occupies.

Formulae and Data

Circumference of a Circle

$C = \pi \times d$
where: C = circumference, $\pi = 3.14$, d = diameter

Diameter of a Circle

Diameter (d) of a circle $= \dfrac{\text{circumference}}{\pi\,(3.14)}$

Area

Area = length $\times$ breadth and is given in square units
$\quad = l \times b$

Volume of a Cube

Volume of a cube = length $\times$ width $\times$ height and is given in cubic units
$\quad = l \times w \times h$

Volume of a Cylinder

Volume of cylinder (V_c) $= \pi\,(3.14) \times r^2\,(\text{radius} \times \text{radius}) \times \text{height}$
$\quad V_c = \pi \times r^2 \times h$

Times Tables

1

1 × 1 = 1
2 × 1 = 2
3 × 1 = 3
4 × 1 = 4
5 × 1 = 5
6 × 1 = 6
7 × 1 = 7
8 × 1 = 8
9 × 1 = 9
10 × 1 = 10
11 × 1 = 11
12 × 1 = 12

2

1 × 2 = 2
2 × 2 = 4
3 × 2 = 6
4 × 2 = 8
5 × 2 = 10
6 × 2 = 12
7 × 2 = 14
8 × 2 = 16
9 × 2 = 18
10 × 2 = 20
11 × 2 = 22
12 × 2 = 24

3

1 × 3 = 3
2 × 3 = 6
3 × 3 = 9
4 × 3 = 12
5 × 3 = 15
6 × 3 = 18
7 × 3 = 21
8 × 3 = 24
9 × 3 = 27
10 × 3 = 30
11 × 3 = 33
12 × 3 = 36

4

1 × 4 = 4
2 × 4 = 8
3 × 4 = 12
4 × 4 = 16
5 × 4 = 20
6 × 4 = 24
7 × 4 = 28
8 × 4 = 32
9 × 4 = 36
10 × 4 = 40
11 × 4 = 44
12 × 4 = 48

5

1 × 5 = 5
2 × 5 = 10
3 × 5 = 15
4 × 5 = 20
5 × 5 = 25
6 × 5 = 30
7 × 5 = 35
8 × 5 = 40
9 × 5 = 45
10 × 5 = 50
11 × 5 = 55
12 × 5 = 60

6

1 × 6 = 6
2 × 6 = 12
3 × 6 = 18
4 × 6 = 24
5 × 6 = 30
6 × 6 = 36
7 × 6 = 42
8 × 6 = 48
9 × 6 = 54
10 × 6 = 60
11 × 6 = 66
12 × 6 = 72

7

1 × 7 = 7
2 × 7 = 14
3 × 7 = 21
4 × 7 = 28
5 × 7 = 35
6 × 7 = 42
7 × 7 = 49
8 × 7 = 56
9 × 7 = 63
10 × 7 = 70
11 × 7 = 77
12 × 7 = 84

8

1 × 8 = 8
2 × 8 = 16
3 × 8 = 24
4 × 8 = 32
5 × 8 = 40
6 × 8 = 48
7 × 8 = 56
8 × 8 = 64
9 × 8 = 72
10 × 8 = 80
11 × 8 = 88
12 × 8 = 96

9

1 × 9 = 9
2 × 9 = 18
3 × 9 = 27
4 × 9 = 36
5 × 9 = 45
6 × 9 = 54
7 × 9 = 63
8 × 9 = 72
9 × 9 = 81
10 × 9 = 90
11 × 9 = 99
12 × 9 = 108

10

1 × 10 = 10
2 × 10 = 20
3 × 10 = 30
4 × 10 = 40
5 × 10 = 50
6 × 10 = 60
7 × 10 = 70
8 × 10 = 80
9 × 10 = 90
10 × 10 = 100
11 × 10 = 110
12 × 10 = 120

11

1 × 11 = 11
2 × 11 = 22
3 × 11 = 33
4 × 11 = 44
5 × 11 = 55
6 × 11 = 66
7 × 11 = 77
8 × 11 = 88
9 × 11 = 99
10 × 11 = 110
11 × 11 = 121
12 × 11 = 132

12

1 × 12 = 12
2 × 12 = 24
3 × 12 = 36
4 × 12 = 48
5 × 12 = 60
6 × 12 = 72
7 × 12 = 84
8 × 12 = 96
9 × 12 = 108
10 × 12 = 120
11 × 12 = 132
12 × 12 = 144

Multiplication Grid and Conversion Charts

×	1	2	3	4	5	6	7	8	9	10	11	12
1	1	2	3	4	5	6	7	8	9	10	11	12
2	2	4	6	8	10	12	14	16	18	20	22	24
3	3	6	9	12	15	18	21	24	27	30	33	36
4	4	8	12	16	20	24	28	32	36	40	44	48
5	5	10	15	20	25	30	35	40	45	50	55	60
6	6	12	18	24	30	36	42	48	54	60	66	72
7	7	14	21	28	35	42	49	56	63	70	77	84
8	8	16	24	32	40	48	56	64	72	80	88	96
9	9	18	27	36	45	54	63	72	81	90	99	108
10	10	20	30	40	50	60	70	80	90	100	110	120
11	11	22	33	44	55	66	77	88	99	110	121	132
12	12	24	36	48	60	72	84	96	108	120	132	144

Distance		
1 inch	= 2.54 centimetres	= 25.4 millimetres
1 foot	= 0.305 metre	= 30.5 centimetres
1 yard	= 0.9244 metres	
1 mile	= 1.61 kilometres	= 5280 feet
1 kilometre	= 1000 metres	= 0.6214 mile
1 metre	= 100 centimetres	= 1000 millimetres
1 metre	= 3.28 feet	
1 centimetre	= 0.3937 inch	= 10 millimetres
1 millimetre	= 0.039 inch	= 0.1 centimetre
1 micron	= 10^{-4} centimetre	= 10^{-5} metre
10^{-6} metre	= 1 micrometre	
Volume		
1 kilolitre	= 1000 litres	= 1 cubic metre
1 litre	= 1000 millilitres	= 1000 cc
1 millilitre	= 1 cc (exactly 1.000027 cc)	
1 fluid ounce	= 29.57 millilitres	
1 US gallon	= 3.785 litres	
1 Imperial gallon	= 4.546 litres	
Weight		
1 kilogram	= 1000 grams	= 2.2 pounds
1 gram	= 1000 milligrams	= 0.035 ounce
1 milligram	= 1000 micrograms	= 0.001 gram
1 microgram	= 10^{-6} grams	= 0.001 milligram
1 nanogram	= 10^{-9} grams	= 0.001 microgram
1 pound	= 0.45 kilogram	= 16 ounces
1 ounce	= 28.35 grams	

To access the Answer Guide for Maths and English for Retail follow these simple steps:

1) Copy the following link into your web browser:

http://www.cengagebrain.co.uk/shop/isbn/9781408083086

2) Click on the Free Study Tools Link.

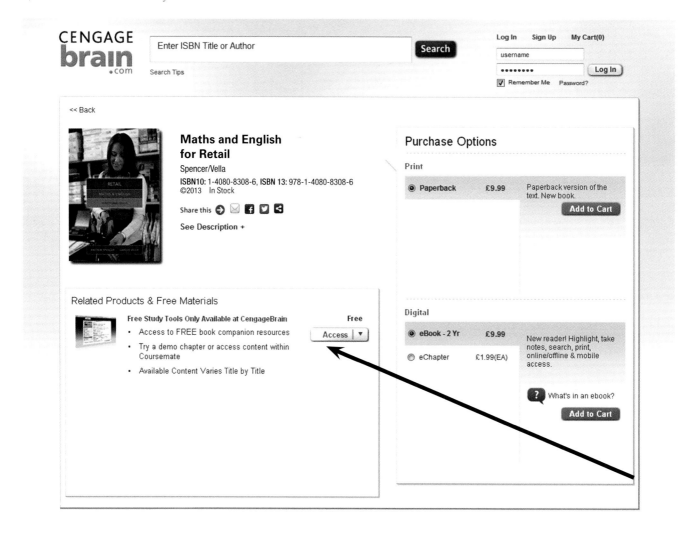

Notes

Notes

Notes

Notes

Notes

Notes